The Confessions of a Reluctant Mystic

The search for the hidden Christ in an ordinary life

SUE TALBOT

Marshall Pickering

Marshall Morgan and Scott
Marshall Pickering
3 Beggarwood Lane, Basingstoke, Hants RG23 7LP, UK

First published in 1986 by
Marshall Morgan and Scott Publications Ltd
Part of the Marshall Pickering Holdings Group
A subsidiary of the Zondervan Corporation

British Library CIP Data

Talbot, Sue
Confessions of a reluctant mystic: the search for the hidden Christ in an ordinary life.
1. Mysticism
I. Title
248.2'2'0924 BV5082.2

ISBN 0-551-01384-2

Text Set in Plantin by Brian Robinson, Buckingham
Printed in Great Britain by Anchor Brendon Ltd, Tiptree, Essex.

Contents

Dedication

To Rhona and John Mayhew . . . to Jenny Cooke . . . and to Joan Ford . . .
Thanks.

Acknowledgements

'Aubade' by Philip Larkin is reproduced by kind permission of the Trustees and Executors of the Philip Larkin Estate.

'Ten little girls from school are we' by Evangeline Patterson is reproduced by permission.

Quotations from *Psychological Reflections* by Karl Jüng are reproduced by permission of Routledge and Kegan Paul.

Foreword

Why should I write a book? Why should I have the audacity to put so many words on paper and think they may be worth the reading? Why should you spend time listening in to those words; these thoughts and experiences sent out into the unknown?

Well, partly I suppose, because books have been real friends to me, alongside the human kind. Sometimes those books have been like a beacon flaring in the night showing me a way ahead. The men and women who have spent all those hours sharing their lives and thoughts with me, a stranger, an unknown and unseen face, have shared something that is from the core: the essence of mind and self. I know I have been infinitely the richer, because they invited me through those words on paper, sent out to unknown lives of which I was and am one, to listen in to what they have learnt of living . . .

So why do I write? Why *this* book? Perhaps it is because I want to keep faith, to keep faith with the light beyond the night, even when the night is dark and full of cloud and the stars are hidden.

Behind the writing and the words is the attempt to keep faith with the mystery of an ordinary life; I attempt with difficulty, with all the strength that is in me, to understand that life and to come to some sort of terms with it. In some way this book is also a keeping faith with the search for the Holy Grail. Over the years—being maybe halfway through a life now—I have had glimpses of the light that can shine out from the ordinary and the commonplace . . . and in that light, all is holy and nothing is without meaning . . .

And so I search with all my strength and with all the breath that is in me, to know . . . Is this so and is it true?

Because if that light is true and no illusion then all lives have their place in the pattern; all lives are special, no matter how outwardly insignificant, how unknown, and if this be true, then so is my own.

So I will keep faith with the vision and the question that haunts me and perhaps in the journey and in the search of an ordinary life; in its pain and in its particularity, that is both like and unlike any other, you may find something that shines out for yourself.

Author's Preface

This is the story, in part, of a father and a daughter. Of a father, who in being a father is like all fathers with a daughter or a son and who is yet himself, like no other . . . of a father who held within himself a shadow that over the years grew to eclipse the sun and in whose darkness his wife and children were shadowed in a web of despair that threatened to drag them down to destruction. In breaking free from that web has come a different life with the shadow now behind us, yet still there; there to be reckoned with.

There was a time, for many years a time, when I wished that I had a father like the father of the images, strong and kind and proud of me, his daughter. It was not to be. For many years I struggled to exorcise the shadow that was within him, that frowned and hunched on my horizon. Then I discovered to my dismay, that the shadow on the outside was within me too.

So this is the story of the search to know and understand the shadow—the shadow that comes within the mind and heart, that holds within itself the potential to destroy even life itself, if we let it. But in seeking to understand we can overcome; the understanding somehow, strangely, bringing us the possibility to be free, if we choose, if we want. It is not always as we think. To be free can be a lonely business and quite unsettling—out there on the moors with the wind blowing in your hair—it can be exhilarating or cold. One can turn into the wind, facing its strength, daring to look straight at the rain-washed skies, the hurtling clouds and the breathing silence, or in fear we may turn back . . . to our eternal loss.

So in seeking to escape the shadow I have had to confront my own and name it as mine. But in that knowing and in that seeking has come perhaps a little of knowledge; a little of wisdom; the beginnings of seeing. And that search and that seeing and the desire to know has shaped my life; a shaping that was and is often painful and frequently unexpected. The wind blew hard and cold and was not to be ignored, sometimes behind me and sometimes in front. The changes of direction are quite disquieting. It seems it was determined that I would not get settled. I quite fancied the quiet life, with a good book and a cup of cocoa. Then when I'd just got myself all set up, the wind would rise on that inner horizon and the sun would go in, and in that growing dark I knew I was summoned to search on.

I don't think there are answers in this book, much though I have longed for them, sometimes with the physical craving of the weary for sleep. But although I cannot in all honesty give you answers, I can tell you of the responses I have had from the questions I have asked that breathing silence. I can describe the inner and outer landscape I have walked through, the beginnings of resolutions to the tangles and questions I have had to deal with; the challenges that have been thrown at my feet.

So where to begin? Where do beginnings begin? Not always where you think nor are they always in the expected places.

Chapter 1

For want of a better place, I will begin with a prayer, which in some ways, considering the quest, is not inappropriate. But it was and is a prayer that was more than itself: a prayer said by many, by law and by custom in a polished school hall that smelt of sunshine and linoleum and carbolic soap. It was a prayer that was a challenge, a problem and a question. And what on earth—or in heaven—(but I didn't believe in heaven, so that place could not be resorted to for help) was I to do with it? This prayer of the Gentiles, that I listened to every day: this prayer with its startling, heart-shaking, unbelievable assertion right at its beginning.

'Our Father who art in heaven . . .'

You see what I mean by beginnings not being where you expected them! I mean, how on earth could you make such a statement? This was no beginning. In many ways it was an ending: the claim to have discovered the Tree of Life or the Philosopher's Stone that turned all to gold. Here was this absurd, this mind-boggling, bold, fantastical, simple assertion . . . and what was I to do with it? I didn't know and so remained silent, listening, thinking, asking questions.

Questions—what a spiky, uncomfortable pack of them. They tweaked and poked and prodded and tore, like a dog, worrying at a bone that it will not let go. They did not let go, my questions. They tug away at my feet and sleeves demanding to be followed. They do not give up. Many's a time I have given up on them, but back they come, tug, tug . . . poke, poke . . . it's time to be on the move again. If you desert us, we will not desert you. You can't get rid of us that easy. Drat them!

'We will not let you go! . . .' Now who said something like that?

A memory shyly inches forward into sight. 'I will not let you go except you bless me . . .' Jacob said that wrestling with the angel.

What good is that to me? I look crossly at the words remembered from reading from the Scrolls. What good is that to me? I am not surprised the memory was shy to come forward. What good is that to me? I know now . . . but that is many years, oh, so many years on. Why are we so deaf? Oh woe, another question. Before my unruly pack get out of hand completely I will move on and listen again to that prayer in that sun-filled hall. So the beginning will, at last, in one way at least begin . . .

'Our Father, who art in heaven,
hallowed be thy name . . .'

The unthinking incantation wound its way to the ceiling tiles of the new school of which I was a proud and fearful member. So many new faces; a sea of faces, a positive tide and torrent, that flowed down seemingly endless, highly-polished corridors. The current of these faces atop of their regulation grey-cladding, swept this one, small, rather fat, outwardly puddingy child, past door after mysterious door all leading to mysteries that I could only guess at. Sometimes smells were an interesting guide but not always. In one room of smells, whose closed door I dared to open, highly polished equipment glared from behind glass cases. Rubber pipes coiled in waiting on silent obedient wood.

The smell was not inviting. I decided to close the door on it.

The school was a new glass and concrete box, an experimental box, for those who were neither quick nor slow . . . a fox-trot box . . . slow, slow, quick-quick, slow; for those in the second band of a tripartite system, defunct now, like the dodo. I was a second child, so in some ways, if not in others, it was appropriate. It was a gleaming box, with bright, sunshine yellow squares included in its concrete steel and glass. Yellow, the colour of the sun and warmth. I was always cold as a child, cold sometimes outside and in. I was glad the school had yellow patches on its dress. Yellow, the colour of the sun; the colour of summer's light.

I was glad it was yellow. It was a proud box. It stood straight and proud against the horizon. It was there and unashamed. It was a foursquare box, with no nonsense about it; no higgledy-piggledy awkward corners; no messing about. It was a very modern box. If you took the lid off, you could see all sorts of smaller boxes arranged inside it; smaller boxes with doors in one side, all neat and in geometric rows, standing in obedient and regular lines along ruler-straight corridors. And the doors, the holes in the walls, could open and shut. These holes in the walls, covered with wood, so that they got renamed doors, could open and shut. Just imagine, opening and shutting holes in walls. And what did these holes in the walls let in and out? Ah, there's the rub, for any nice, neat regulation, obedient box: the holes in the walls let people in and out. Or at least people in the making. Otherwise known as children but living, breathing human beings all the same. The trouble with human beings is that they are all higgledy-piggledy with awkward corners and lots of messing about. In many ways they are highly inappropriate contents for a neat and tidy box. Still, in its way it was a friendly box. It did what it could. In some ways it changed my life, or rather the life that went on inside it did. I certainly have never been the same since. But I suppose in some ways that is true of all of us, all the time in one way or another. Still, I'm ever so grateful to that gleaming, sun-yellow-harlequin-squared box: my school. In a way it saved my life. I will never forget it.

Schooldays: no, they were not the happiest days of my life, but they were a refuge, a haven of predictability and routine that was safe, because of its sameness. You knew what was coming. Well, at least most of the time you did. What others hated, I welcomed with relief. The boredom-scarred desk invited an escape; it spoke of protection and a partial defence against the unknown. Behind a desk I knew what was expected. The desk was a kingdom, small, but a kingdom all the same. And a kingdom—even a very, very, small one—is worthy of a certain pride. I gloried in its neatness: books, brown-paper embraced, labelled and layered in obedient piles; pencil-case, polished, docile, awaited my attention, eager to help me in my studies. I wished that other parts of life could be so neatly and conveniently ordered, but wishing, unlike in my much-loved fairy stories, did not help. My life at home had a different, disturbing, darker, oh, so much darker pattern. It made me shiver with the cold of it. Shiver inside and out.

'Our Father, who art in heaven,
hallowed be thy name,
thy kingdom come,
thy will be done; in earth as it is in heaven.
give us this day our daily bread . . .'

I listened; I had to listen, because I was there . . . and not somewhere else. Now that's an interesting thought . . . All sorts of things grow out of being in one sort of 'there' and not another.

So I listened, the outsider, to this prayer: this prayer of

the Gentiles. I knew as I listened that it was a dutiful saying of a prayer of habit. How did I know? How do we know any such things? Because, of course, I had also said years-full of prayers of habit, of unbelief, of duty. So I recognised its tone. One can usually distinguish the dead from the living.

As I listened to the shape and colour of this prayer, said by so many, given a kind of breath by so many lips, I wonder if it is not said as an incantation at times: a prayer of magic that will somehow make the world go right, that will ward off the evil eye, when it glares in our direction.

This prayer . . . what a prayer! What a claim! What a demand! A demand for the kingdom of God to be brought to earth. As a Jew, I had not always seen concern for the kingdom of goodness to prevail against the desire to mock the outsider and to feel the stronger and the safer for such mocking. And I should know—it happened to me.

Even now, now I am on the inside and can say those words, those startling words—when I feel strong enough—even now, now I am on the inside it has happened to me. But it is for different reasons, I think, or perhaps it is in some ways the same. Just that I am different and yet just the same; the outsider on the inside; the stranger within the gates—and as such dangerous.

'Our Father, who art in heaven . . .'

These words, so over-familiar to my classmates, so unfamiliar to myself; what did they mean?

'Our Father, our *Father*.' There were so many fathers represented here: human fathers, who like the mothers, carried with their title the image of the ideal in the spoken word.

Father, the Strong One; the Provider; the Hunter, the one who defends his family from danger and hurt; the source of food and home. 'Father'; the Protector; one on whom to lean—so the legend ran.

Funny how fathers have often destroyed food and home and become both the danger and the hurt. They do so, not always in the guise of father, but it is done all the same. I wonder why and do they know it? Are they inwardly blind when they say the cruel word that cannot be then unsaid, when they give the blow that will scar the inner and outer self, when they walk away and never come back?

What do they see, these fathers: these fathers with the guns, when they mow down life; a man with his family on the steps of a church; a woman with her children in the enemy village? What do they see, these fathers with the dead all around them and even in their own home? What do they see? I do not know . . .

I looked at the grey-coated ranks of girls, pressed into a superficial similarity by the demanded uniformity of dress. Deluded by this sameness that hid the twists and knots of our diversity, I pictured the homes behind the daughters. After all I was young. It takes a while to see beyond the surface. The surface can be a safe place to be. At least you know what it looks like. The top layer looks like what it looks like, is what it is.

Now I am older I have sometimes chosen not to see, not to look behind the mask at the hidden depth and if I did choose to begin the risky business of considering the underneath of things, it was certainly not until I was good and ready. The journey to the centre takes a considerable amount of energy if not downright courage . . . and I for one have always been reasonably convinced that I am a coward. Now and then I comfort myself with the thought that perhaps true bravery is to be afraid, really afraid: the knee-quaking, dry-mouthed, sick-in-the-stomach kind of fear, and still to endeavour to face in the right direction at least. But I'm not always convinced. Perhaps it all depends on where one is going.

Still innocent, if not naïve, I pictured the homes that

stood behind these daughters. All had gentle mothers, and fathers proud and strong, who looked with pride at their daughters. Now I know better, but then I thought it was only I who was caught and held in knots and tangles not of my own choosing; knots and shadows that tore at my mind and heart.

It wasn't always so. My father, once upon a time, was real. He was a father like others: one who laughed, who hummed a happy tune whilst driving; a father who proudly, chest forward like a robin, with all his feathers fluffed out, walked beside his son down suburban streets. He was then a father who teased and tickled and talked.

* * *

I remember sitting, feet swinging in space. The shiny wood of a pew in front of me; the synagogue light and airy, and garnet-red shadows glinting on the silk threads of the prayer shawl that I plaited and unplaited through my fingers: my father's prayer shawl. I was a girl. There was no prayer shawl for a girl.

The silken threads fell and trickled through my fingers. I would play with them for hours or what seemed like hours, until the pages of the solemn, black-backed book were turned and I saw the large black type announce this end of an hour in another world. The word 'sermon' was the tolling of the bell. Soon after the plaintive cry of the choir, the incantation of the Hebrew liturgy would be quietly folded away and be put back on the bookshelf, till the next weekend had been reached.

My father stood beside my brother, the fruit of his body by his side. We stood to attention, solemn and quiet, no fidgeting now as the Scrolls of the Law were carried heavily by in tinkling procession. The silver bells with which they were adorned swung gaily to and fro but the atmosphere was not of carnival and festivity. It was a very serious thing, this passing of the Law. The silence held and turned my body, whilst the cry of the choir was like the cry of the gulls over the barren wastes of the seas. Yet there was an exultation in that cry and a triumph. A triumph, that the wild, high seas had boundaries, that the dark that threatened to flow in upon us and within us was kept at bay by the sentinels, the Scrolls, held upright: proud and singular and very old. They were held by living men, walking round the boundaries of our estate, our selves: our living, breathing bodies. It was the shadow without and the shadow within that was bound by the Law in its passing and in our acknowledgement and our reverence for those Scrolls, who were its guardians.

Boys with straight, still faces stretched forward, hand wrapped in their prayer shawls to touch the silver plate, that swung beneath the tinkling bells. Reverently, they would kiss the shawl that touched the scroll. My brother when his time came, took his place, made for him by that very Law, which he so carefully, so gently touched. He took his place in the line of bodies of boys, who leaned forward from beside their fathers, leaning body bent to touch the Law and be blessed, then upright again by their father's side. Father and son: in synagogue they were father and son and so the line went on. In that special place they were father and son, side by side . . . in synagogue but nowhere else. I looked at my brother as I waited, waited for the passing of the Scrolls. What did he feel in that, his special place? I did not know. I do not know. No girl leaned forward to touch the silver bells, to kiss the Law. Here we had no place.

'Shalom.'
'Shabbat Shalom!'

But was it peace and is there peace, outside or in? The Law was behind the gates. We walked slowly through the greetings, through their wishes and their hope, my father and his son and myself. The rabbi dressed in black. Why are all religious men in the West dressed in funeral black? What do we bury? He wished us Peace and nodded and smiled to see a father with his children by his side. To see a man bring his little ones to the Law and the reading of the prophets was good, the smile said. We were nodded out, standing amidst the Saturday-dressed-best of Manchester Jewry, secure amidst our own kind, as busy shoppers scurried by.

It was always with my father that we went to synagogue. After all, it was the man who stood before the Law; it was the man who would take his place amidst the Assembly. It was the boy who stood forth to take his place, when his time came to be a man, so it was with my father that we went. My mother came, sometimes, but she was happier at home, Queen of the House, centre of our lives. It was to mother that we returned.

Chapter 2

Once a year there came a time that was special, very special. It was a time full of a flock of smells, that appetisingly wheeled and flowed through the kitchen—the hub of the home. (Perhaps that's why people always seem to gravitate to kitchens, and conversations can grow around its table. I've got to know lots of people in kitchens.) The house smelt of happiness.

Amongst the clutter and the patterned chaos we prepared for *Pesach*, the Passover; my mother and I. My colleagues from school were looking for Easter eggs. We also would have an egg at our special table, but it would be burnt, the marks of the flames left upon it.

But for me this time was a good time. There was chopping and boiling and roasting and that flock of lovely smells wheeling around us. Mum would potter happily in and out of the kitchen, sugary hands texturing her gaily coloured apron, cleaning out tins for their new load of special Passover fare—cinnamon balls, plump and round and cheeky, puffing out their chest in rows and clusters amidst a dusting of icing sugar. The almond cake sat damply waiting our hungry attention. But best of all was the deep, rich-brown aroma of heaped raisins, simmering their way to raisin wine, their fragrance filling the house.

'Chop, chop, chop, thump, thump,' went the knife as I chopped apples and almonds to make the symbolic *charoseth*, which represented the mortar with which the slaves in Egypt used to make their bricks. The bitter herbs were simple parsley, press-ganged into a different service. Soaked in home-made brine it tasted most unlike itself, poor thing. In our house we made two kinds of bitter herb and not only once a year. The second sort you could not see.

Here, my mother and I were close; here in the warm, bubbling, simmering quiet. Here, I felt a necessary part of the whole. Yet even here amidst love and care carried by the scent of baking and simmering wine, the darkness slid through the open door.

The front door banged. Heavy feet trod in. The weight and rhythm of it swung like the tolling of a bell. Did my father hear that warning toll, telling of an end to come? I think not. We heard it and thought it only tolled the end of a happy morning. We were right, but the bell had begun to toll for more than the day.

He was a big man, my father. Big-made with large, wide shoulders. Tall and solid; a body you could have leaned on in a gale. I wished he'd listened to the message of his body. It would have been good to have had a father you could have leaned on in a gale, big and solid, with roots that spread wide, that no tugging wind would dislodge. His body has withstood all sorts of shocks . . . the bolts of electric current convulsing it . . . the push of insulin sending it to sleep, chemicals as many and various as an alchemist's dream, and still it battles on past stroke and alcohol, but seeming now only to house a world of shadow.

Bang. Thud, went the kitchen door. My father's big body stood in the space of the pushed back door. He did not smile.

'What the bloody hell is that!' The lips curled round the snarl.

My mother's face looked bewildered and her shoulders hunched as if against driving rain.

'A lamb bone . . .'

'Well, take the bloody thing back! It's no damn good! Don't you damn well know what the proper thing looks like after all these bloody years?'

My mother's shoulders straightened. She stood up and looked that scowling, bitter face in the eye.

'What does it matter, Ralph? What does it matter . . . It's a symbol, just a symbol, a bit of bone. Does it really matter which bit of bone? Does it really matter?'

For once the twisting mouth had no reply.

I was exultant but also afraid. What would happen next?

The two looked at each other.

Nothing happened.

He went away and the door banged shut. The thud, thud of the feet going up the stairs had a different sound, a very weary sound. An upstairs door banged to, behind the sound of the feet. Then all was still, except for the thudding of my heart. Bump, bump, bump, bump, it went. Anyone would have thought it had been running a race, stupid thing. Maybe it had. But if it had I wasn't at all sure of what race I was in. I found that out later.

Months passed and another year opened a door to this night, this special night.

Seder night . . . a special night, this 'night that was unlike all other nights'. That's what it said in the book, the special book for the special night. It said that this night was different from all other nights. I knew. I had read it. I asked the ritual question that asked the question I wanted to ask.

It was rare that the questions I wanted to ask and the questions that I was supposed to ask so conveniently coincided. The answer answered the question; that should have been that, but it wasn't.

The answer said that this night was different from all other nights, because it was on this night that we remembered the 'Almighty, Blessed be He, who brought us out of Egypt, with a strong Hand and an outstretched arm . . .'

He brought us out of slavery and oppression and cruelty. That was the answer, that's what it said. Well, it matched. There was a question and there was an answer. The two balanced each other. But why, oh why, was I not answered? I was not answered because behind the ritual questions were so many more. They were packed so tight I was afraid to unloose the one. Where would it end? Where indeed? I was right to be afraid. The questions struggle on. They have shaped my life.

Have we hope of answers before the long sleep and our awakening; to know what there is to know? Perhaps . . . John Hick, the philosopher, has said, 'Christianity is verifiable if true but not falsifiable if false.' When we die we will know what there is to know . . . or nothing at all. Are there answers to the questions we ask on special nights, when the dark presses close? Perhaps. Perhaps beginnings, beginnings of answers, a chink of light through the crack in the door.

My father washed his big-man's hands, big, square, man's hands; 'a strong man's hands,' said his hands. My brother and I watched these big man's hands wash in a cut-glass, glinting bowl. This was a washing that was different. The cut-glass, curving bowl pronounced it. Now, why should my father wash hands that were already clean? I saw that they were clean, pink and white clean. Now why should a father wash hands that were already clean in a bowl normally reserved for the special-occasion trifle? . . . a bowl that shone and glinted its own cleanliness to the scrubbed and waiting air. For once I had the sense not to ask that question. I knew that the probably reply, 'Well, that's what's written; that's what you're supposed to do. It's in the book . . .' would not somehow be worth the asking for.

My feet swung to a silent beat under the table. The tale, the ancient tale was beginning to unwind along its fated course. Soon the time would come for the question, the special question, my question, which was three in one, a triple cluster. I waited my turn, the turn of the youngest. Sometimes it was fun to be the youngest, not often, but sometimes youngest could mean special—once a year maybe.

One should not ask too many questions. It can get to be habit, a dangerous habit: you never know where it might lead.

'Why is this night different from all other nights?' I proudly spoke the traditional words. The first of the three questions asked by the youngest in the family. The first of the three questions asked was general. The others followed on its heels, worrying at the main question, demanding more details, more specifics. . . . Why do this and this, why exactly was this night different from all other nights? The traditional words were there, waiting for me. They were my words given me as of right. They waited all year for me, these questions. They needed my voice, my bones and blood and breath to speak them: I the youngest. I was so proud. I had waited for them too, these questions that were mine.

But it is dangerous to ask even ritual questions, for behind the ritual question is always a real one, and where there's smoke there can come a fire.

I was to realise that even here, strengthened by my special place on this special night, there was no rest from the questions that were beginning to worry so worryingly at my heels. These words I spoke were mine only because I happened to be the youngest. They were borrowed by birthright; they were not really my own. Unless of course even one's place in the order of birth has its own significance, its part in the pattern.

'Why is this night different from all other nights?' My ten-year-old voice rang proud and clear, too definite for the small horizons of a small, suburban semi, its twelve-foot floors and white-painted walls barricading out the night, though it came in nonetheless. The ritual questions and answers brought the night from the outside to the inside. Perhaps it is always dangerous to ask questions.

'Why is this night different from all other nights?'

'Because our forefathers were slaves in the land of Egypt, until the Lord, with a strong hand and a mighty arm led us out of bondage, Blessed be He.'

My father's voice carried the unknown tones of generations layered within it. For a moment he had the strength of his body, of such bodies that have withstood the force of the storm, for a moment, for a borrowed moment, for this night that was not like other nights. As he spoke the answer I could hear his father say it to him, his son, as his father had said it to his children and his father's father before him, stretching back into the mist of the past from generation to generation, until it reached the generation from which the tale had sprung.

'In every generation there arises a Pharoah who seeks to destroy the children of Israel . . .'

There was a silence. It hung waiting.

Bent heads examined the lightly burnt *matzot* lying so stiffly on their backs on the bleached-bone-white plates. We tasted the bitter herbs of the outside variety: the transformed, humble parsley in its salt-soaked brine. With the tasting came knowledge and memory: bitter images of yellow stars, smoking, stinking chimneys, black leather and walking skeletons, whose eyes lived nightmares.

In every generation there arises a Pharoah. Would there be one in my time, I wondered? Somewhere, someone didn't like us. That dislike could feed and grow fat on fears, ignorance and dreams. It could and did sometimes turn into a ravenous hunger, the hunger for the scapegoat, to know the enemy who was on the outside, to identify and kill them: a hunger for blood to be poured on an altar. It was strange to be so labelled, to be a Jew.

Now I am older and know a little more of living, I know there is always a Pharoah, in each generation a Pharoah who seeks to kill the children of God, but the children of God wear many names: the dissidents in Russia, Steve Biko, Martin Luther King . . . the list is endless, the journals of Amnesty International record just a few. The rest are known only to the invisible God, no matter the unmarked grave in which they died. But wherever a human being has the courage and vision to speak out against tyranny and injustice, against the cruelty of the eye and hand and voice, the light in the night shines. And still, yet still against all odds, the night has not put it out. The men and women who give it voice may be put in jail, shot, exiled or tortured, yet still it speaks, that still small voice: the incarnated voice of God. And all the Pharoahs of the world have not yet silenced it.

What is it like to be a Jew? To wear that particular label to the world. The word somehow has within it the sound of the yellow star. 'A Jew . . . You're a Jew!'

Why did it so often sound like an insult? Jewish was all right; just an adjective, like French or British, but Jew . . . 'You're a Jew' . . . felt like a slap across the eyes. I still flinch, when I hear that label spoken . . . 'You a Jew?' 'Yes, I'm Jewish . . .' I answer.

So much left unsaid.

What is it to be a Jew? Ask two Jews what it is to be a Jew and you'll get three opinions, or so my father said.

To be head of the household, descendant of a long line of a race that has survived by the very traditions that have marked it out as different, can be a source of strength, when your own flame flickers low. And so it was for my father, for a while. 'I am a Jew,' was said with pride. It straightened the back. It was a flag to fly against the wind.

I can see him now at the Passover table, the shadow

indeed having passed over for a while; resplendent in his dark suit, freshly shaven, his big, wide, strong-body's-shoulders embraced by the white and blue striped-silk-tasselled prayer shawl: a coronation robe. Tonight he was the father, head of the house.

The service round the table wound on its way. The question of the youngest child now being over I meandered through the minutes by looking at all the pictures in the prayer book. The ones of the ten plagues were the best. They were the most exciting. Things were happening in the pictures of the ten plagues. Here was action, not talk, except for the last one. The last one was different. The last one drew me back again and again until I stopped and looked it straight in the eye; like a rabbit caught in the light of a headlamp, afraid and fascinated I could not look away. The last one was of the aftermath of dying. Its stillness was a pool and my looking the pebble. The ripples went out and out.

I had been drawn once before towards a circle of dying. I was playing in the garden, an ordinary garden full of city-grey-dappled laurel leaves and bedraggled rhododendron bushes. There was a crash and a squeal of brakes and then I saw it. It came staggering and weaving its agonised, drunken circle into our drive. It lurched and swung on pain-splinted legs that had lost their living quality. They looked like legs of wood covered in matted, bedraggled fur. It wove its death agony, round and round, round and round: a hypnotic desperate-dervish dance. My horrified gaze was dragged along with it.

Inch by unwilling inch my feet followed my eyes. It was a nightmare come to life: a horror had walked into my world.

'Please God, make it stop. May this stiff-legged staggering stop.'

It did.

The circle was broken but not the horror and its magic

draw. Inch by inch my feet went to look. What did I see? Just a dead cat? Just? What did I see? I looked at death for the first time that afternoon in the garden of the grey-dappled-city laurel leaves. I saw the look of death and knew, knew even then that it was utterly different from a living being. That whatever life was it was not here . . . and that perhaps dying was different from what was left over afterwards. It looked so very much *not* like a cat. A dead cat was so very, very different, something so very much other and so very un-cat-like.

It was my very first lesson and I never forgot it. One has to begin somewhere.

This last picture, the last plague of all, was such a simple thing, an old-fashioned line drawing in pen and ink. But what it pointed to was not simple at all—shocking rather. It showed rooms looking out onto other windows through which you saw other rooms and in them all a dead child, a boy sprawled all higgledy-piggledy askew across a bed. And a woman weeping in the hole of the door.

Now I am older I know that it is usually men, soldier men who do such things. It is usually the work of war and revolution. But here was no gun, no bomb's blast. It was the 'slaying of the first-born'.

I have a first-born son.

The stillness in that picture put out a cold finger. What would it be like to live in a city in which every family had lost their first-born son? The weeping must have beaten down the streets and shaken the very stones of the houses.

The lamb's bone that had made my father so angry sat modestly and innocently on its own plate, the shadow now forgotten, the tolling of the bell silenced by the power of this night like no other.

The special book said that the blood of the lamb that was put on the doorposts of the house made the angel of death pass over. The angel of the Lord saw the blood upon the door . . . But why, why should blood stains save the first-born son? Did you feel the angel of the Lord pass over? Would it have been like a coldness across the moon—a cold that stopped the hearts of those who slept within unmarked doors?

Would you, could you see the angel of Death coming, as people had seen visions of other angels in other times and in other places? The simple drawing gave no clue. It was a question that I knew could not be asked on the outside. It was a question that would have its answer but on the inside. It was not when I expected it, nor at a time that I would have thought would have had anything in it connecting it to the picture that held me in its grip. It was at a birth, the birth of a first-born son, that I began to sense the beginnings of what it was like, but that was to be for me, not him. It was at my son's beginning that it came. But it was not for now . . . not yet.

Life is full of surprises.

Slowly one gets acclimatised to being astonished.

Chapter 3

Apart from that special night, 'that is different from all others', there are two other festivals that are special, central and crucial in the Jewish Year. The three together are the trinity of the Old Covenant, perhaps of all covenants of the mystic way. In the one, the night when it is remembered that the Angel of Death passed over, it is at the symbol of the letting out of life that death stops. The blood, the life-blood-stain, guards the threshold and protects the first-born son from the shadow that passes over. The following two are closely linked together in time and theme. The celebration of the New Year: life going on, the renewal of the seed-time and harvest, of winter and summer and the life that springs from within dead root and sleeping seeds—a time of new beginnings. Closely, inextricably bound up with the time of new beginnings is the Day of Atonement, when in fasting and silence and ritual prayer the way forward, on the inside and in the outer world, is cleansed; the way made clear for the new life to flow, a clearer stream. When the way is cleared it is then that we can be at one with the spirit within, and the Life from which it comes and that life in others. It is not for nothing we talk of the need for atonement.

But for me as a child of ten or twelve, New Year meant only one thing. I waited, for once patiently, for the moment of magic to come. Time and again I would strain in my seat to see the wrinkled-parchment-yellow horn, twisted and silent, lying in its contorted circle on the polished desk of the rabbi. Slowly, the service wound its way to this moment, when the Saturday quiet of the synagogue would be split by the tearing shriek of the ram's horn, the *shofar*.

Teckeeeeeeeeeah . . . Teckeeeeeeeeeah.

A horn was lifted up. You could see the man tensing all his muscles, drawing up the column of his body's strength; the flesh drawn in round the air held so carefully within the ribs and stomach. Then all the muscles, cords and sinews of the neck and face standing out with the effort of sending out that blast of warning, that shriek of air; the note created by an agony of pressure from within the dead coil of shuffled-off horn.

Teckeeeeeeeeeah . . . Teckeeeeeeeeeah.

Its braying sound discordantly beat against the polished respectable doors of a place of worship. It wasn't at all a respectable sound. It was real, that sound; real and strong and frightening. I wonder if the real thing is always like that: real and strong and frightening and utterly, completely, unrespectable.

The note was high and taut, straining the ears. It created a tight band of sound that was cut by the sudden sharp silences between the notes. Two short, sharp, spluttering cries and then a long, warning shout . . . of danger, or threat or victory . . .? I could not tell.

Then, a desert war: a sun that glared and beat upon the brain, dying men in twisted heaps who looked at last on a man's hand and a ram's horn lifted against the sky; now, the hand was clad in a city, business suit, the skin unscarred, a homburg hat above the silken prayer shawl.

*　　　*　　　*

If you invoke a God be careful, He just might answer and, as the prayer book says, the God of Abraham, Isaac and Jacob is not the God of the dead but of the living and He never slumbers nor sleeps. Really a rational person can't be too careful. Fortunately for the peace of our materialist minds, the powers asleep in symbol and liturgy do not often awake. But God is not mocked. The mystery that they proclaim, the symbols and liturgy can become power conductors for the very thing they point towards. Religion's dangerous stuff. The real thing, that is.

I spoke to a rabbi the other day. A true rabbi, a lover of the lore and law of his people. He had been drawn into an experience, willy-nilly, almost without a by-your-leave. He did not really choose it, it chose him. 'I have always regarded myself as a rational man' . . . the tone was sad, regretful for a lost certainty and safety. Two men drawn into a ritual beyond the ritual, that three years on, they still do not fully comprehend or understand . . . What unleashed this power within the ritual? It was the blowing of the ram's horn, in the Days of Awe before the High Holy days of the Jewish people commence. A call that should have lasted seconds, repeated; demanding the two leaders of the service to continue, because this call of alarm and warning was not, it seemed, finished. So the rabbi called, the *shofar* calls, and the caller blew the trumpet. The alarm was sounded. On and on they called, drawn to the Ark, the centre of the service and keeper of the Scrolls. The two men thought they had called the ancient calls of the *shafar* for maybe fifteen minutes extra to what had been intended . . . When they looked at their watches it was an hour and forty minutes later. The call had called itself through them.

But have we the ears to hear and understand the nature of the alarm that has gone out? The spiritual world needs as much exploring and research as do the deeps of inter-stellar space. Maybe the world inside is as big as the world outside. But for the inner voyage we may need different tools and equipment.

*　　　　　　*　　　　　　*

Can you imagine a child not wanting to eat? Not because it wasn't well, or because the food offered was repulsive to it, no, for no other reason than that the child wanted to experience the experience of not eating. Not eating from choice has a grander name—fasting. Perhaps it is one of the tools we need for the inner voyage to the continents within. The old books say so and the old books can tell us a thing or two now and then. My brother fasted, all day, like the men . . . and the women. The grown-ups one day a year didn't eat. Imagine! They didn't eat breakfast or dinner and only had tea when the sun had gone down. Twenty-four hours of no food! No toast, no chocolate, no meat or potatoes, no apples or pears. Nothing.

My brother didn't eat. So he must be like the men, 'grown-up', but he looked not *that* much bigger than me . . . to me. When did you stop being a child? When did you cross over the line? Growing up was a funny thing to do. It happened to you and mostly when you weren't looking. Others decided when it had happened and how fast, or so I decided. My brother always seemed to grow faster than I did.

Now I am older I feel younger than when I was young. When I was young I felt older; odd that. Perhaps it takes till we die truly to grow up. Perhaps we neither can nor should ultimately grow up. It is an interesting experiment to discover what is possible and what is desirable about this 'growing up'. In some ways I grow to believe in it less and less. In other ways I think or rather feel it as a life-long task that is always a little beyond me but infinitely worth aiming for.

I remember my brother going with my father, hand in hand, proudly pacing down the pavement; man and boy on their way to a concert. I could not go. I wasn't old enough, they said. When I was older, then I could go, when I was grown up. I didn't feel as little as I looked. I knew I looked little. I certainly looked little when I stood against my brother. I came to his chest or thereabouts I think. I looked quite little in a mirror. I knew what little looked like and I knew I looked right for little. The word fitted. Well it fitted the outside. But I didn't feel little on the inside. And oh, I did want to hear that music and hold the other hand of my father and go to this grown-up thing called a concert. It sounded so definite, so there-ish. A thing to be discovered.

I waited anxiously to be more grown-up. Would I know when I was? I waited for a long time, day after day, week after week I waited, yet the time never came. I never went hand in hand with my father and brother to hear the music play.

A year turned upon a year and upon a year.

The big school had welcomed me into its friendly boxes. I was a big girl now. I could join the big people and eat nothing for a whole day. I could experience this act called 'to fast'. It sounded so solemn, so very serious, so important. Perhaps it was, perhaps it is, more than we think, this way of praying with the body . . . but that took many, many more years to discover and it was discovered from the inside, not from the rules and the lore, although the lore speaks true. Mind you, the outside experience has its uses, hinting and nudging at the mind and heart, telling you that something is 'there' waiting for you to discover it from the other route, when the time is right. When it's its Time.

Yom Kippur had come. It was time, or rather the beginning of its time. This year I would go and fast in the synagogue. The day had come after all.

If you forgot . . . you did grow up unawares and were surprised.

From the balcony I watched the sea of hats below, moving and swaying to the rhythm of the service. Smiles had been left at home. We stood at limp attention as the service chanted its way through the day. There was no shriek of a ram's horn here to command attention. Ritual prayer was heaped upon ritual prayer, layer upon layer. The minutes were pressed into hours. Then the hours were pushed aside as we walked out into the sharp, bright, autumn day into the city streets, blinking like moles in the sunlight.

It was dinner time but no dinner. I didn't feel as awful as I expected or as different. There certainly was a lightness in the stomach and the head! I was cold. Mind you, I was always cold, inside and out usually. Today, colder on the inside—the outside, in the crush of the High Holy days, was quite warm.

It seemed wrong somehow to be window-gazing on a Day of Atonement. It was too ordinary, too commercial, too vain. Where was one to look? I tried seriously to contemplate the Manchester pavements. They did not inspire. So I looked at the faces and well-dressed bodies of Manchester Reform Jewry. The faces smiled and nodded in greeting and agreement, in recognition and support. 'Yes, we also are here, upholding the Law, observing the rituals, fulfilling our destiny.' Why then did it feel as if there was no centre?

After half an hour of walking nowhere and resolutely gazing at nothing in particular, we returned to the dusty, silence-filled interior of the great hall.

Now the minutes developed size and length. They fed on our growing weakness and flaunted their endurance, so slowly they moved. I tried to visualise them as fat, wheezing, Tweedledum figures. I felt like kicking their behinds to make them move a little faster. Well, it made a change from counting sheep. The other possibility was to count hats. Hats were required by law and custom. I never was told why but that was nothing new. 'Why' comes in so many varieties and is so demanding to answer, I can well understand now why it causes the bravest and strongest of those deemed 'grown-up' to quail at the sight and sound of it. I've been on both sides of that 'why?' now, had a good look at it back and front . . . Life is quite just at times.

Time slowly tick-tocked itself away. The hats nodded and swayed. I lost count after the fiftieth petalled hat. Now here was a strange thing; we were here to bewail our sins, whatever *they* were, to be sad, sorrowful and repentant and there were the hats, full of flowers and colour and laughter . . . spring-like hats, hats that applauded the trees in blossom and the fields in flower. What were the heads beneath the hats thinking? There was no way of telling. What would we have for tea? Perhaps we would have roast chicken or *gefilte* fish? Six o'clock was a generation away.

I had fasted now for nearly twenty-four hours. I had been sure I would feel so different. I did not. Time staggered by. My stomach rumbled and squeaked its protest at missing its second meal of the day. I wondered if my neighbours in the pew could hear my, as yet only biological, protest. I hoped not. It was embarrassing.

A day was coming when the beginnings of a new kind of existence and experience would begin by protest: a negation that grew into an affirmation. It would be a protest, a challenge and a question: the triple cluster that set my feet on a long and sharp-stoned road. It was a road that was also an adventure, full of strange views. But the time was not ready and the moment of rebellion was hidden in the folds of years yet to be lived. Hats, not surprisingly, was its ostensible beginning, the beginning that was the beginning of an ending, but not yet quite the beginning of the beginning. This was the ante-room.

We were praying to be forgiven, but to whom or what? The time-worn prayers had a beauty of sea-worn rock but the edge was blurred.

'Sin!' . . . Now there is a strange word. Was it the same as crime, as naughtiness, as evil? My head ached with the effort of trying to decipher the code, my stomach ached with its long emptiness. When I shouted at my brother was that a sin? What if he had started it by putting on the 'Big-brother-routine'? What about not wanting to give in . . . and the slamming of doors, not once but twice and three times, each one louder until the wood shook? Was that sin? Then there was yelling at my brother when I lost a game . . . again. But perhaps big brothers should start with a handicap at Monopoly and chess? I mean three and a half years was bound to give you an enormous advantage, wasn't it? God was supposed to be awfully keen on fairness, wasn't He? But was fairness the same as the 'Justice' that kept cropping up in the readings said amongst the hats below? I wasn't too sure.

'Honour thy father and mother, that thy days may be long in the land that the Lord thy God has given thee.'

I was accused. 'Honour thy father and mother' . . . Always . . . at all times . . . no matter what? There were no words read out to parents . . . 'Be worthy of Honour!' I would have read them out, while I was young I would have read them out. Now I am a parent, thinking of my father in his shadow, I still ask the question. But I begin to understand that just to survive may at times be worthy of honour. It all depends what is the nature of the shadows that haunt us. What is their strength and what is the nature of the light that we are given?

But why, why is it only to the child, that the command is given? It wasn't fair! My accusation rose weak and feeble to the ceiling and fell with a silent squish to the floor. I picked it up to examine it further. What was honour? Was it love, respect, admiration? Well, I could do that sometimes.

The Scrolls, heavy and thick, were thrust upright into the waiting air. The man's hand shook with the weight, the arm taut, the muscles stiff and strained under the Saturday suit. The music rose to greet the giving of the Law. Slowly, stiffly, the parchment scrolls were lowered at arm's length to the rabbi's desk. I wondered whether the man would drop them. He looked as if he might but he didn't. I was a bit disappointed.

Chapter 4

David, a father, wept at the death and ruin of his son Absalom. The death came before the dying. You can hear it in the cry of anguish at the final ending of hope; a cry for all that could have been and wasn't. It was a cry of all endings, of all dyings; the loss of hope of the light, the hope that there can or will be any other beginning ever again, in this life or beyond it.

'Oh my son, my son, Absalom my son . . .'

The king covered his face and the king cried with a loud voice, 'Oh my son Absalom, Oh Absalom, my son, my son!'

He wept for a son, for a son lost. He wept for a usurper, a son who sought to kill a father. So the victory of the people and the saving of the king was turned to mourning, for the death of a lost son.

The tie of blood is stronger and stranger than steel. It binds us in ways that astonish and defy reason.

Sometimes it needs the inner strength and visionary sight of a true leader to challenge that bondage of blood, from which we need to be unloosed if we are ever to walk free upon this troubled earth. And yet if we cannot love our own, can we love truly anyone? It is not an easy balance to achieve. In the end we all choose our own way and live out the consequences of those choices. Yet there are times when the way is complex enough without the bands of blood pulling us back into grief and ambivalence, so that we are like the king, whose captain had to rouse him by the truth, a truth that was an accusation and a command . . .

> ' "You love those who hate you and hate those who love you. . . . for today I perceive that if Absalom were alive and all of us were dead today, then you would be pleased. Now, therefore arise, go out and speak kindly to your servants; for I swear by the Lord, if you do not go, not a man will stay with you this night; and this will be worse for you than all the evil that has come upon you from your youth until now." Then the king arose and took his seat in the gate.' (2 Sam. 19:6-7)

The truth is distinctly disturbing. It takes quite a bit of adjusting to, a reorientation of the mind and heart. But he did it, the king—and the new beginning was saved.

When I remember that story I hear the cry of the father for the child gone astray, for the son lost. But where is the cry of the child, the child wandering in the inside world of shadow for a father lost? A child now grown, weeping for a father who did not weep for her. Where in the old records is the cry of the daughter mourning for the mother? Where is the cry of the daughter, wandering the world looking for a mother lost in the land of the dead: the reversal of Demeter and Persephone?

The king of the dead is within us.

There are many who need the music of Orpheus to summon them forth from the land of the dead. But once we are on the journey towards the upper land, towards the light, let us not look back. If we do look back we cannot say that we have not been warned.

But there is always a morning before the night and always, after the night, the dawn comes. As in the seasons of the external world, so in the inner seasons of our spirits.

In the memory of my father there are glints and sparks of light in the dark. Light that is within the shadow but not beyond it. But perhaps this distinction is more apparent than real. Light is light wherever it is to be found . . . and like the light from the sun it has within it the capacity to touch all living things and promote their growth.

I was not at all surprised recently to read that the Maudsley Hospital in London has done some experiments in relation to 'seasonal depression'. They had noticed that for some people depression was lifted in the spring. They exposed some patients to strong light, the same intensity as of a bright spring day, for up to three hours before dawn and the same period after dusk. The patients had to do nothing at all apart from be awake in the extra light. These sessions were to begin in the autumn with the waning of the natural light. All of the patients improved with the light treatment, some dramatically. The average change was sufficient to bring patients from a state in which a normal life would be impossible to one in which they could cope with a demanding professional job. Dim light had no such effect. The Maudsley trials would seem to link the darkness of the mind with similar changes of behaviour linked with hibernation..

It is interesting how what is intangible has so much power. Concentrate light, and the human mind can be enlightened, not in the intellect, but from the mind to the heart. Concentrate that light even more narrowly and it can cut through steel. What is new and what is ancient come together. The laser and the first creative act mentioned in Genesis . . . 'In the beginning God' . . . and when the spirit of God moved upon the face of the deep, there being no form and only darkness covering the depths, the first creative command was 'Let there be light!'

By what do we measure the immeasurable distances of space, but by light and the time that that light takes to reach us. What is central to the theories of relativity that have so altered our conception of our Universe, but light and its central role in the three and four dimensions.

But it is in the dark that the power of the light is made most clear.

The tiny flame of the night-light can alter the world for a sick child or one who is sick at the heart, if not in the body. I well understand now, the impulse to light a candle for the dead, that it may shine beyond the world, linking the two dimensions together . . . the seen and the unseen. I have lit a candle myself sometimes, a special candle for me, for me and my son; a candle to defy the dark . . . a light against the shadows.

So I remember the light in the night of my father.

My father was the active one in our family, always glad to be out and doing . . . That is, he was glad to be out and doing when the shadow within and beyond him hadn't literally flattened him onto his back, so that he stared with unseeing eyes in a darkened bedroom where it was always made to be night.

Day after day, month after month, he lay on his back. Pills arraying the mantlepiece, multi-coloured bits of chemical to rearrange the feelings in his head. Rainbow-bits of manufactured hope in bottles and jars, a modern alchemist's shop. But the alchemist's dream of turning base metal into gold is not achieved so easily. The chemical path cannot lead us to the pot of gold, the crock of happiness at the end of the rainbow. I chased a rainbow once, mindful of the story of the treasure. It was always in the next field and the nearer you got to its end or its beginning, the more the colours were indistinguishable, fading against the solidity of the rough-tough grass. The pretty rainbow chemicals can offer us relief, but they do not show us the way through the shadow; they just blur it a bit, blunt the pain so that we can carry on a little easier in our breathing. But the centre is not changed.

For the changing of the centre, we have to listen in a different way to the wisdom of the fairy stories, but that I didn't realise for many a year.

Fairy stories fascinated and haunted me. I read them voraciously, munching through maybe six or eight books in a week. Curled in a corner I read and read, lost in the worlds summoned up by their magic, and safe for a while from the menace of my own. Unknowing I was taught by them, the patterns and images laid down on the bed of the river. They were to surface unexpectedly, coming to my aid when I least expected, as I travelled on the inward way. The inner life is as full of surprises as the outer one. You need all the courage and the simplicity of the youngest son of the ancient tales to deal with the dangers and setbacks of both worlds. But it was in the tales of the land of Faery that I first felt the call of the wild . . . the wind blowing in from the Celestial City: the approach of the Other . . .

So my father slept, in the day, through the day and through the night. We were amazed at his sleeping. The clocks ticked by. Hour after hungry hour was sent away empty, unlived. Time slid by. Week after week passed in the shadow . . . and then we were out. Out of the tunnel and into the sunlight, and we all breathed a little easier. Without apparent rhyme or reason the grey pall over the house was lifted and we were on the move.

It was with my father that we went walking and exploring. Both of these treats usually occurred on holiday.

When I look back I see two images of my parents on holidays. My mother is sitting by the pool, or on the seashore, lost in her beloved books, lost to the world I am inhabiting. My brother and myself are digging with great care and precision in the smooth sands, digging under the expert advice of my father. We are making a boat: a boat, that wonder of wonders, you could sit in, a boat of sand with a little seat and room for your legs, a boat of sand, neatly and carefully and lovingly made. It was a boat that had a seat for sitting in to wait for the tide to come in. It was a lovely boat. I can see it still. But the trouble with a boat of sand is that it doesn't last. It dissolves in the tide. The boat in the mind doesn't though. The boat in the mind lasts through the years and glints in the shallows.

It was with my father that we built the cars and the boats of sand. . . . It was with my father that my brother and I rambled slowly with no particular purpose along winding roads and up breathless hills. It was my father who said, 'Oh, we're nearly home now . . .'. But the 'nearly' could last a sweat-dripping hour or two. The nearly was not nearly as near as one could wish.

I have found that since. The effort to get from 'nearly' there, to the actual end of the journey, which usually turns out to be the beginning of the next, can be very great indeed! It's not for nothing that there's talk of not looking back, when once you have begun and your hand's to the plough. Once you begin, you can find that you are on a road that is very much longer than you anticipated; that there are turns and twists in its length that you could not see from its beginning. . . . Still, perhaps it's worth the odd blister and aching, breathless chest to get to the end of the road. Endings can be very satisfying and not at all frightening. The view from the top can blow your breath away with its beauty—the landscape of sky and mountain range. The way down can make the legs ache with the effort of keeping the balance, but at the end is the bowl of steaming soup and a bun, smelling of home.

It was with my father that my brother and I built the inevitable sandcastles and fortresses that alternated with the much-loved cars and boats. From those castles of sand and shell we learnt together, my brother and I, the lessons in them for all children; the learning to accept mortality and the transience of life, through the symbol of sand. We watched, fascinated and grave, as the ramparts crumbled away under the slow, insistent, smooth tongue of the sea.

It was with my father that I went to the stone-wrapped water's edge, to skim stones. I could watch and try for hours, longing for the moment when the stone, flung from the hand, would skip on tip-toe across the smooth sliding surface of the sea. It was such a happy skip, like the bound of a squirrel up a tree. Oh and that I had made the stone skip, that it had skipped for me, dancing so fast across the waves, that was good indeed!

Father and daughter stood side by side on that sea's edge. Father and daughter stand still on my inner horizons, looking at the tide coming in, listening to the waves roar.

Then my father exhorted and commanded me to fill my aching, asthma-filled chest with that special air, sea air, full of 'ozone', so he said. He was always sure it would do me good, like medicine. But the medicine I needed was the medicine of the skipping stones that danced across the sea.

Now in that inner world, as we stand and watch the tide come in, drawing with it the night and the waning of the light, I know I must search for a while alone for the light beyond the night, before that night comes to shut his eyes. I must find that light for myself, so that I can say to him, standing watching with fear the incoming darkness of the waters, that 'it's always darkest before the dawn . . .'. So I can say 'I know', because I've seen it—the light coming beyond the night sky. We only perhaps have to wait for it, and turn, turn from the tide's approach and look.

Funny . . . you wouldn't expect to learn an essential lesson in the pattern of living in a hotel swimming pool at a little seaside resort. It's amazing what's tucked away in the ordinary and commonplace. With the loss of colour of some of the hairs of my head I begin to see a little clearer, and what I see leaves me open-mouthed. My first experience of fear left me open-mouthed too . . . a mouth open and gasping in panic. I was a mere nine or thereabouts . . . a girl who loved to swim for hours, lying back and enjoying the mind-boggling fact that this permeable stuff could actually hold you up—if you could dare to trust in such a miraculous and difficult-to-believe-in fact. One should sink, but one didn't, as long as you believed it, that was. If you doubted, you sank. It's a very religious experience . . . swimming.

My father had taken me swimming, my mother at the pool's edge happily tucked into a deckchair with a book for company. The sun shone, the water glinted; life was good. Happy splutterings and gurglings, laughter and shouts, filled the sun and salt-filled air. All was going well. It was a large pool in comparison to the pool at home. It was extra wide at the middle. I coasted happily along and then, unmindful of the significance of the action, in the middle of the pool I got tired and tried to put my foot down.

That was when the mouth-open, gulping-clasping bit began. And they weren't happy gasps either. The bottom wasn't there, or rather it was there but twelve feet under! I was in the deep end without knowing it. The middle, in this con-man of a pool, was the deep end. The realisation that I could not put my food down in a place where I had expected to be safe, brought a panic that could have drowned me. Interesting that . . . the fear of the unexpected problem is the cause of the overwhelming, not the fact itself. I could swim. What did it matter if the bottom was four feet or six feet or even twelve feet below? If you could swim you were safe; the water held you up. You did not drown.

But panic stopped all that. Panic meant I stopped believing. I stopped believing in the experienced fact. I could not reach the bottom. I could not rest. I began to sink, gulping and gasping, with the sea-water closing over my head. I had not breath to call. Panic stiffens the body, the arms flail, the back like a rod, a lightning conductor for disaster.

How did he know, my father, that his daughter desperately

needed help? I don't know. I did not ask. All I know is . . . it came. It was enough.

That big, strong-man's body, already a little too cocooned in flesh, came to rescue the spluttering, gulping girl. Strong hands calmed the panic and held me still. Interestingly, he didn't immediately take me to the shallow end, but there in that terrifying depth he taught me how to deal with such a crisis—what to do when you're out of your depth and you can't put your foot down.

Rest . . . rest and use the techniques you have learnt . . . and with them rest, rest on the surface of the water. Lie back and it will hold you up. Mark time by treading water . . . anything that helps until you have got your breath back and can begin again, swimming back to a point that you can cope with. It was a good lesson in survival. Later, much later, I was to need that lesson in a very different context.

It has taken years to realise that it is our resistance to the feared fact that is the problem. The resistance and the fear breed the tension that can break us. When I dare to turn around, having got my second breath to look at this fearsome fact staring me in the face, it can be surprising what I see. Sometimes there is a trickle of light round the edges of the shadow, a hint that there's something else hiding at the back of it . . . but only there for the curious, for those tantalised by the glimpse. But unlike with Tantalus, the son of Zeus, condemned to see both food and drink just out of his reach, that glimpse of light at the back of the fear, beyond and behind the shadow that threatens us, is there to draw us on to its discovery. Life needs a lot of courage. The Mount Everest can be on the inside.

When we know that, there can come an inner call, an inner call from without; a call to move beyond the known and the safe, where you knew where the bottom was, where you knew you could get back to the solidity of land; where you knew where you stood.

I wish my father had learnt the lesson he began to teach me in that swimming pool of long ago. He has lain down under the tide and the waters have rolled over his head.

*   *   *

There are two special times I will always remember with my father. They are warm, like an amber stone, filled with liquid honey; warm and sweet and when held to the light, warm to the touch, no matter how cold the weather.

When my mother's birthday crept towards us, my father and I would walk hand in hand, in secret—or so I thought—to the shops. My pockets sagged wearily, full of carefully hoarded pennies. Laboriously, with great seriousness, I would count them one by one into the assistant's hand. My father would confer with her in whispered undertones.

'Let me help you count them . . .' he said, gently holding the remainder of my hoard in his big, man's hand. Always my so carefully hoarded savings came to the right amount . . . always.

On one occasion I chose a cup, a precious cup inscribed with flowers, pink and pretty; a symbol both for the words I was not old enough to think of or say, and of what my mother represented. She made life delicate, to be treasured, warm and conforting like tea.

Now, when I think of my mother I think of her in a warm-furry-pink dressing-gown, wrapped and folded round the middle like a cosy, food-bearing bear, the Mummy Bear of all the best fairy stories, whose porridge is too sweet. I had difficulty with the mix of my own porridge's flavour, but that is the story of Little Bear and that chapter comes later in the story.

It's not for nothing that my brother and I call my mother 'Pink Momma' sometimes. There isn't the red-hot power and passion of the blues of the Black Mommas, but in that image is all the warmth of the creation of the home within the home . . . the nest-maker, the one that lines the harsh bones of the twigs with fluff and feathers . . . the maker of *lockshen* soup with dumplings—the giver of treats and hugs.

At Art College once I was asked to put a colour to various loaded words, one inevitably being 'sex'. . . . I made the warmest pink, a dye that shone transluscent too. The lecturer came and stood behind the shoulder of the girl bent over the pigment shining on the paper.

'Why pink? Why pink for sex . . . and that pink?' he asked.

His voice was quiet and very puzzled. Of all the words, I knew that was the one that would be inquired about . . . inevitable really. But perhaps it was the colour. I wondered what colour he would have found appropriate. I described the feeling of the 'Pink Momma'. He went away shaking his head, bemused.

The cup I wanted to buy was pink, pink and pretty. Oh how much I wanted to buy that cup! That cup would be just right. It was a very grown-up cup. It was not a child's gift; it was grown-up, a proper cup. She could not fail to know it was special; so delicate it was, with its elegantly soft, curved handle and gold rim. Just in case, it had MOTHER engraved at the centre of its heart in flowing script. I could not wait to see her face when she unwrapped the shyly smiling cup and saucer from its tissue. She did love that cup . . . she has it still.

I did not see my father's secret smile to the assistant nor her replying gentle look, as they watched the solemn child, so tightly embracing its mother's special cup, gingerly circumnavigating the doors.

I didn't see the smile, but I remember and in remembering am thankful. It is a help, an ease to the pain of the shadow that lingers, hunched in his room; an old man now . . . old outside and in.

Strange that in the pattern of things it was my father who taught me to be still. One of the greatest treats of my childhood was to be allowed to listen to the music my father loved. I wonder what it is in music that keeps the black waters at bay. King Saul, all those centuries and centuries ago, knew it and asked for the young boy David to come and play the music that banished the black tide in his mind.

My father, although no king, recognised that truth and used music constantly, to keep the shadow at bay. But I was young and unaware; a girl of five or six. Scrubbed and shining from the bath I would be allowed to sit at his feet, back resting against the solid sofa, soaking in the sounds that danced around the room in time with the flickering of the firelight shadows against the walls. It was a magic time—a special time. I was right about the magic.

Seven years later, I summoned up that magic time again. I was in great need of magic, my feet encased in elephantine plaster; the hospital bed raised so high in an effort to stop the bleeding that I was in grave danger of falling off on to my head! Home was geographically far away. With pain drumming in my bones, lonely and homesick, I summoned up the genii of home. I lay and remembered those fire-lit nights. I chose to forget that the fire lit in those nights was dying. I shut my mind like a door against the knowledge that knocked for entrance, the knowing that the warmth I remembered, the warmth that was on the inside was eaten away until only the shell was left. But it was a real memory linked with a truth that had been alive, and that life warmed me through the long, pain-filled night.

I wrote and asked my mother how 'things' were? But she never answered. Not that she didn't reply. She wrote all right. But it was as if the real question had never been asked. We do children a grave injustice in not giving them the truth, the right response to their question. The covering is done from kindness and a desire to make their way easier, but the fiction covering the fact only causes confusion and the tension of unease. And in the end, facts cannot be evaded. They are there . . . they will be bumped into sooner or later . . . one way or another.

My mother was good at writing chatty letters, pages of cheery sounds on paper. I lay on the hard, wood-slatted hospital bed and wondered what was really going on. I lay and looked inside at the fire-lit image of home. But I knew. I knew from the silence of what was not said and from the sick-cold in my stomach that the fire had gone out.

Later I found out that my father had taken another overdose and been rushed in a bell-clanging ambulance drive to have his stomach forcibly washed clean and empty. The black tide had sucked him away.

Chapter 5

My father in one hospital bed and I in another . . . an interesting correspondence that . . . I immobilised by crooked but now broken and realigned feet: a girl with enormous legs that would soon be encased in elephantine boots, complete with squeak! He, immobilised by a breaking on the inside, out of reach of X-ray and operating knife. Both in our separate beds we waited for another day.

The day came; it usually does.

It brought a nurse in blue, the day did. Days are full of surprises, tucked away in the odd corner. She had come to make my feet respectable. Did you know that feet could fail to be respectable? They can . . . they can. The trouble with my feet was that they had bled too much. The ugly, angry red stain had spread and spread, darker and wider: a spider of blood reaching to the edges of the neat-white plaster of Paris barricades. The wood-slatted hospital bed had been raised and raised at the foot, presumably so that the escaping blood would find the trek too much of an uphill climb. For a while I was afraid of sliding off the top on to my head! The blood eventually took the hint and decided that the uphill climb was too much bother, so it desisted and returned to its usual routine. Our bodies can be surprisingly obedient. But the stain was there, dull, hot and angry. All was not as it had been.

The nurse brought a large, battered tin bowl, crunched and munched at the edges. She put down a neat roll of bandages, a stiff, white, plaster of Paris butter-curl. The neat, scrubbed hands carefully and slowly uncurled the stiff roll of hospital butter. She soaked the roll in the tepid water, the little pond in the battered tin growing murky with its grey-white swirls of plaster dust. Layer by careful, mathematical layer, the red-blood-spider was banished. Under its cocoon of white it went underground to growl in the night, reminding me with force at times that unseen was not to mean ignored. Still, the bandages did the trick with their stiff, white cope. All was now well, controlled and neat. Neat and tidy and in order . . . manageable. My feet would now not embarrass by their excess of blood. I was now passed as suitable for going home.

Only a few more hours in this world of pain and pills and polished linoleum. A few more hours to forget the night I remembered more than all other nights—'Why is this night different from all other nights?' says the youngest child at the Passover table . . . I knew why this night of all nights was different from all other nights. It was the night I lay and listened to the battle for a life.

Through the night it went, the calling of the name: a human voice calling to the life behind the name to come back . . . come back.

Behind the shuttered screens the call went out.

It was quiet, but the carefully breathing bodies of a ward of children lay and listened.

'Marie . . . Marie, Marie, can you hear me?'

'Marie, can you cough? Try and cough.'

'Marie, Marie, can you hear me?'

'Marie . . . Marie . . .'

Surely, surely she would hear. We certainly could. That calling voice held us still through the hours, with its tireless, commanding plea. The gentle power and drive of that voice I hear still.

'Marie, Marie . . . Can you hear me?'

'Marie, can you cough . . . Try and cough, Marie . . .'
'Marie . . . Marie . . .'

Surely, surely, she would hear, wherever she was, wherever she had gone to. She would hear and come back. My ears ached with the effort of listening for a reply. It never came. The call was sent tirelessly out. Through the hours it went on and into my troubled dreams. Eventually I slept; one usually does.

With the five o'clock light twenty pairs of eyes looked towards Marie's bed. There was a gap in the neat symmetry of the ward. A gap and a question but the question was never asked, or at least not by me, not then. The nurses bustled, as was their wont. The battered bowls of tin did their usual rounds for the cleaning of the teeth and face. Breakfast duly came and went. It was as if the night had never been. Soon the gap was filled by a new bed and a new, small, breathing body. All was back to orderly normality. But the gap and the question lived on.

When I had left the world of tepid water in battered tin bowls and the plaster and the pain, the only letter I ever wrote to a girl still in the ward, a girl whose face is now blurred and faded by time, asked her how Marie was? . . . what had happened to her? For some reason I desperately wanted to know. What had happened mattered. I needed to know which way the battle had gone . . . it was all I wanted to know. A letter came. It said she had not died that night. In time they had called her back. I sighed with relief. It was enough. I can still see the once hunched, twisted back and young, so old, so old face of Marie. Her back will be straight and tall now. I still hear that call sent out and am glad, glad it was heard.

Oh the power of the love and strength and persistence of the unknown doctor who called! The power of the name that drew her back!

I ask a different question now. I look for a different

answer. But the questions, the impact and the weight of them held me first that night. It had begun in the fascinated stare of a child at a wounded, agonised cat, circling to its tortured death. It came near to my bed that long night but it had not come yet for me, only near me. But perhaps the two are not so different.

What was dying all about? What was it like on the inside? Where did you go to? Where did you come back from? Was there some 'from' from which to travel backwards towards the present I lived in? It made your head ache.

A girl with the legs and feet of an ill-made statue examined the memories of home, school, parents, brother and friends. No, no one had spoken of such things. But the thing was to be looked at. It was there, the question incarnate on the opposite hospital bed. Marie . . . she might know. But I never met Marie again, her part in the pattern being now complete. But living it is different from looking at it.

That night that was like no other night made me look and search through all the school-filled years for something, somewhere that might help lighten the heavy fear. It held us as breathing, still statues of skin and bone and blood: living images, breathing children pinned into stillness by fear and a question; stiff, straight lines underneath the hospital sheets.

No, I could recall no whisper, no echo that would help me through the long, long night. It was fortunate for me that I was only looking and listening, not having to live my way through that particular question.

RE lessons—there perhaps help would be found, tucked neatly and tidily in amongst the too-familiar stories. When I looked inside at what was left of my RE lessons, all I heard was a high-pitched voice . . .

'Good morning, Form Two.'

But the tone did not fit the greeting, nor I think did the

face and life behind the voice find the morning good. Mind you, facing our class, who could blame her? A year or two later we managed to convince a student teacher or two that teaching was not for them. We were rather proud of that sorry fact, feeling and flexing the muscles of our power. Perhaps we did those two unfortunate teachers-to-be a favour . . . perhaps they found a pattern that was kinder to them than we had been. I hope so. One day I was to face a class that knew its strength and decided they would take me on to discover of what mettle I was made. I could not say I had not been warned.

On the rigid hospital bed, I looked inside my head at the body that embodied the voice of the RE lesson. The Michelin-tyre-form bounced its way down the aisles of desks, busily explaining that . . .

'You see, Form Two, miracles were only thought to be miracles by primitive man, man without the marvellous aid of science. Now all can be explained . . .'

All?

'All is now clear. When Elijah brought the poor widow's son to life, he was only giving the child the "kiss of life". We do not need the supernatural now; all is quite understandable scientifically . . .'

I see my hand wave, frantic and desperate with thought . . .

'Please . . . Miss . . . Miss . . .' (Why did she not see?)

'Yes, Susan . . .' the voice was resigned.

'Please, Miss, but . . . but they didn't know of artificial respiration then . . . did they? Like you said . . . it wasn't scientific then, was it . . . but he did that all the same . . . without knowing anything about it . . .'

There was a long, hot silence . . .

'So I mean, Miss . . . it was a miracle . . . a sort of miracle . . . because he wouldn't have known what to do, would he, Miss? Perhaps that was the miracle, that he did that, all those years ago, before they knew anything about it . . .?

The silence got hotter, the face got redder.

I could not remember what happened next. Certainly the story of Elijah was dropped and the question quickly covered by a gaily coloured map, I think. A map of the two kingdoms . . . divided into two. Quite apt really . . . when you look at it. My mind is at times too uncomfortably divided into two—the mystic and the sceptic; uneasy bedfellows, but in time I may find a way of their being friends. I'm working on it!

I can't remember a thing that my RE teacher said after that lesson.

On that hospital bed I looked again at my question, examining it carefully from head to tail. It looked a good, healthy question. She should have been pleased with you, I thought, squinting at it again. . . . But it wasn't too much help for the matter in hand . . . the question that was struggling to answer itself in the bed opposite. And so I put it away for a rainy day. I have it still. It is a question like many others that needs its answer to be found.

I looked again inside my head for memories folded in the suitcase of the brain, to see if there was one that would give some clue as to the meaning and outcome of such struggles as the one taking place in the bed across the polished linoleum floor.

What had my rabbi said? There were no words of death and dying that I remembered, no signposts there. There was the memorial service with its ritual chant, men swaying, gently moved by an internal breeze, rocking to and fro, to and fro on the balls of their feet . . . the downward lilt of the end of the chant, '*mimeru,* amen,' hung in the air. What does it say, that phrase . . . 'Let us say amen . . .'? So simple . . . a call also to say, 'So be it . . .'.

But what does it mean . . . this prayer? It is only now, thirty years on, that I have asked for its meaning. There is a different rabbi now—a man with a different sense; a fellow seeker, looking for the divine: a true rabbi. Not all rabbis who have the name are the name in truth. Although I had not known the meaning of the prayer . . . the *Kaddish* . . . I knew, without the words, that beyond the words this was not a prayer that would answer my question. Or at least not in many ways. It is a prayer of praise: a prayer of wonder and amazement at the greatness and otherness of God, the Source of all living things, One who is utterly beyond time and space 'May the greatness of his Being be blessed from eternity to eternity . . . Let us exalt and praise the Holy One, who is beyond all honour and all consolation . . . May great peace from Heaven and the gift of life be granted to us and the family of Israel . . . May He who makes peace in the Heavens grant us peace . . .'.

Traditionally it had begun as a prayer said by rabbis at the conclusion of study, and so it came to be used at the conclusion of a life . . . at the end of our bit of study and experience of our bit of the universe.

But ah me, there was no peace in the face of the silence and the call that went out from behind the National Health screens of the bed by the other wall. I could not say amen . . . I did not know the God who was afar off, I did not know a God who was near at hand. Need is not enough. I am driven to seek to know. Is God? Are all things of meaning?

It has taken twenty years of separation, of following a road that is anathema to the Jew, before I could return, holding both truths, the two together: the teaching of Christ, that a sparrow does not fall without the knowledge of God . . . that all our hairs are counted; and the utter greatness and otherness of the divine. Now I can say, '*imru,* amen . . .'. Like Hamlet I begin to know that there's a special providence in the fall of a sparrow, and that, 'If it is not now, it is to come, if it be not to come, it will be now, if it is not now, yet it will come, . . . the readiness is all . . .'.

The long, long night had passed. All nights pass and are followed by a dawn. The nurse had come and gone. I had respectable feet. My bag was packed. I was ready to go . . . in theory.

I should have been happy. I was going home. After the long, waiting, pain-filled weeks I was going home. I should have been happy. I was not. I re-read my mother's letters.

'We seem to be having such hot weather. I'm quite exhausted by the heat . . . Andy comes in, shirt glued to his back, moaning and complaining about the sun. We're quite a pair, aren't we? Are you enjoying this hot weather? I know you love it. Can you sunbathe in hospital? Someone was telling me down the street that their daughter came back quite brown from your hospital.' And so the chat had trickled on, lines of friendly and loving noise, of greeting. But little else. They did not tell me what I wanted and did not want to know.

'Looking forward to going home now?' the nurse smiled and tweaked a recalcitrant cover into regulation neatness. Her face was puzzled, the smile slipping in front of the child's silence.

I did not know and therefore could not answer. I would find out soon enough one way or another. The discovery of what lay behind the chat of the letter on my lap was only a few hours away.

I wonder why hospitals, which could be places of such love and truth, are so often filled with pretending. Both doctors and patients pretend at times. We do not want the truth so much as we say we do. I pretended. In my thirteen years I had had time to learn the pretending game. The smile was glued on for the weekly family visit. There was no word spoken of the pain that sliced through pills and potions, that made me cry and cry without a by your leave. I could not stop the crying; it went on and on. But if I could not stop it, I would make it silent. It's quite odd having tears dribbling into your ears, the pillow piebald with soggy patches.

We are so ashamed of tears.

We had all pretended, played the masquerade, actors upon a stage, smiling and smiling in the bright, white light of the hospital ward. 'You'll be soon home,' they said, my brother and mother and father. Home . . . home . . . oh how we ache for home. I had dreamed of it, thought of it, pictured it in my head when visiting time came and I was alone: the hospital too far for those from home to come to me each day. All the beds were festooned with brothers, sisters, friends or parents: living bodies that barricaded against the silence.

What would I do without books! Faithful as ever, they were the gate, the door of escape from the bed with no screen of living, breathing bodies telling of home. The bed, my bed, was so bare, so empty, so conspicuous. Behind a book, I went away and only came back when visiting was over. When I did have my family circled round the mitred hospital sheets, there were times when I had the feeling that it was as bare and empty as when there was no one there. You have to be there inside and out for home to be where you are.

They meant so well, my mother, brother, my father: my family . . . and so did I. But the pretending game is dead at the centre. It is at what is real that we must begin . . . what else is there? All else is by-pass meadow. It leads nowhere.

Home . . . I was going home. How the phrase rang like a bell! Home-time; being let out of school, the lessons over. Home of the fire-lit music, the favourite meals. I thought of my Mum and wondered what special dinner we would have tonight. Perhaps roast chicken and roast potatoes, followed by a special treat, Lemon Surprise Pudding, steaming in brown round bowls. Oh what a relief from the white plastic trays and the darkk, brown shrouds of gravy sitting on the hard, grey meat! Then there would be the fire and music and my own bed. The dream had helped warm the long, long nights. Again and again I had put aside the sinking at the centre of the stomach that told me the dream was a dream, past and gone now. But even a dream can be a comfort in the cold of the night, and even the dream had been real once.

I should have guessed. Somewhere I think I knew, but did not want to know . . . and so was only half prepared for what the homecoming was actually going to be like. Still, half a loaf is better than no bread.

My father's battered, brown felt trilby hat advanced towards the bed.

'How are you, Sue?'

'OK.'

I heaved my elephantine legs, their accompanying stick and myself—reluctantly owning all three—from their perch on the high, hospital bed and squeaked my way noisily to the door. The squeak emanated from the hideous-huge orthopaedic boots. 'Stupid old clown boots!' I cursed them in disgusted shame as they squeaked their way slowly, oh so slowly down the shiny floor. My back prickled with stares as I propelled them and myself along with one of my father's old, grey-brown, rubber-tipped walking sticks.

I was going home.

All was well at first.

Carefully shepherded into a hotel *en route* home, with a mother and a father at each side, an impassive, who-cares-about-what-I-look-like look on my face, the squeak and myself got as rapidly as we could to a corner seat shelter. Beneath the dull-dark-glass-topped table, the thick plaster leggings and circus-clown's boots were hidden . . . for half an hour. The table resignedly held up yet another pot of tea and plate of biscuits, while conversation came and went . . . mostly went. The half hour ended, as it had to do, and my body, legs, boots and I heaved our way out of the retreat in the corner seat and jerkily rocked ourselves with the help of the ridges on the soles of the boots, past the carefully-non-staring faces.

The journey home was nearly complete. My father hummed away the miles and hours, happy in some measure now he was at the wheel, but my mother's face was stiff and quiet. The silence was not eased by my eager yet reluctant questions, nor the gentle *résumé* of the news, such as it was, with what should have been the reassuring smallness of day-by-day happenings. In the silence that pressed against my ears, the words that were not spoken clamoured and cried to be heard. Comments and questions flopped to a halt under the weight of the words that were not said. Three stiff faces looked and listened to my father and his toneless humming that rose and fell, a chant without a liturgy, as he drove his daughter home.

I held on tight to the dream for a little while longer. It had been a good dream. I did not want to see it go.

When we got home we would light the lounge fire and Mum would potter happily round the kitchen. There would be a favourite book to find and, although the plaster legs could not be tucked into a corner and sat on in the favourite chair, the book would take me to Narnia again, plaster legs being no obstacle to such inner travel. Then the meal of chicken and Lemon Surprise Pudding, steaming in friendly bowls. There could be no hot bath. It would be weeks before the aching feet could be soaked in gentle water, but it would come, so a hot wash would do for now and then, apple in hand, there would be the listening to the fire-lit music.

What a fool I was! A young and hopeful fool. Head in the sand, I tried to keep it warm. In the end one has to come up for air. The air is part of the real world. In the real world the truth will find us out. Soon, soon I would learn not to dream. But the dream had had its place. When its time was over it was put aside.

True dreams refuse to be put aside—so I have learnt. It is only those that have died and lost their strength that curl up, shrivelled in the light of the day.

The front door clanged to behind us. While putting my bags in my room I heard the heavy thud, thud, of my father's feet up the escape hatch of the stairs. I waited. The shuddering bang of the bedroom door came . . . of course. I should have known. In a way it was a relief to acknowledge that in fact I did know. At some level somewhere I knew. This is how it would be . . . and it was. The dream was over. I never dreamed that dream again.

My brother disappeared to do boyish, brotherish things and my mother's unusually silent form was enclosed in the safe familiarity of kitchen wall. Silence settled like acrid dust on the evening.

What was to be done?

Oh how I longed to shout and scream . . . a fury, a Medea . . . hair long and loose and flying in the gale of my anger. I wanted to shout and stamp and rage and thunder through the house, to break down that blind, deaf door . . .to spit and scream . . . 'Don't you care? Don't you care what you do? I've come home . . . my bones ache and throb. I am so lonely. I dreamed of home, longed and ached and waited for today. I dreamed of a special welcome. I thought you'd all be specially nice . . . today . . . just for today. I would for you . . . if it was you . . . at least I would have tried . . . I thought . . . I thought . . .'

I felt such a fool, a hideous, awkward, plain-Jane fool with white, tree-trunk legs. What was to be done? What could I do? Nothing. I said nothing. Took my plain-Jane self with the white, tree-trunk legs and sat them in the corner chair with a book . . . of course.

My mother's voice slid around the door to find my chair.

'Sue, call your father . . . tea's ready.'

'Dad! Dad!' I yelled, the voice flecked with red, the anger perforce showing through. 'Tea's ready!'

The three of us sat waiting. We studied the china pattern of our plates with great care. We waited for the advent of the shadow. It came. My father, dressed in his usual faded, grubby, smoke-holed dressing-gown, with its golden cord, slammed into the room. I glanced from under my lids at my mother's and brother's faces; they were fixedly non-commital.

'What bloody rubbish is this?'

The urge to throw the carefully, lovingly prepared food full in his growling, complaining face, was almost irresistible . . . almost, but not quite.

Instead I answered him in my head. 'You lie in bed all day long and then have the nerve to complain, I wouldn't cook you a thing!'

Outside there was silence.

I watched my father's lips curl in anger.

'You look like a wolf,' I thought. 'You snarl and spit like an animal, a wild, cruel beast.'

I was glad when that face went out of the room, banging the door behind it. Back to bed again.

I was too young then to ask or think what had made a man so? How was he so reduced and imprisoned in such a darkness? There are reasons for all things, if we can but find them . . . if we want to know enough. If we will but journey to find them, the answers are there to be found, but they may not be what we want. To know is sometimes more uncomfortable than not to know.

So the meal, the special meal, was turned to dust. So it has lain, a dry, grey, bitter thing, covered by the years.

Three inaudible sighs staggered with relief round the table. We ate on, silently, the knives and forkkks clattering. What could be said?

That night sleep came, when it did, stiff as the plaster of Paris and as cold: a cold that the blankets tried in vain to ease. Home was no longer a haven from the storms that might blow. It was here at home where the storms would blow now, cold and angry and dangerous.

Chapter 6

'A rose by any other name would smell as sweet . . .' but would it? I had heard the power of a name to call a living being back. Words are power-packed: layer upon layer of life and experience folded round their core. At the centre is the essence of experience that people through the ages have tried to catch in sound patterns of meaning that can speak across the chasm of time, across space and to the bodies and minds of those still unborn. Whether spoken or read, words live on and change us.

The winds of the storm within the mind of my father blew wild and cold and dangerous. For a while I sheltered from the blast through the haven and the harbour that was the printed word. They seemed safe enough. I should have been warned. As C. S. Lewis, whose Narnia books I so much loved, himself said: 'an atheist can't be too careful in his reading . . . there are books left lying about . . . bibles left open . . .'—the nets and stratagems of the Divine, who I do feel at times is quite unscrupulous. Still, fiction was safe enough. They were only stories, weren't they? And they passed the time away. When the hours plodded by on leaden, clod-hopping feet, a good story made the minutes whizz, and suddenly it was tea and bed without a second thought for the locked door upstairs or the silence that emanated through the solid, silent wood.

In hospital, the girl in the next bed had lent me a book, *Voyage to Venus*, a science fiction story by the author of the much-loved Narnia books. I would read it and the book would get me through another visiting time without visitors. It got me through more than that, and I'm still not exactly recovered from the shock. These stories began a train of thought in my own mind that would lead me on a road that I had never imagined or planned. A road from which there is no going back. All began by signs and symbols, black squiggles on a page. Of course it wasn't only the words. They intermeshed with echoes from the wonder that is the world we walk in, so often unawares.

I am surrounded by wonders and terrors that keep asking me a question. Then I was only thirteen, but I had the feeling without the words, that only many years later did I recognise in the psalmist's cry:

'When I look at thy heavens, the work of thy fingers,
the moon and the stars, which thou hast established;
what is man, that thou are mindful of him,
and the son of man that thou dost care for him?'

(Psalm 8:3–4)

It was just a book, just a story, pictures in the mind, but they began to change my world. What I saw and felt shifted out of focus and began to rearrange itself . . . it was most discomfiting. The new arrangement, the new focus, suggested a world that was perhaps even larger, more mysterious and strange than the one I already inhabited and that even now took my breath away.

What did it say, this story? It spoke of a new planet . . . a world in creation, still forming, hot from the presses of the universe. There was a woman and a man, water and pulsating light, animals and silence and a command that was to be obeyed. A scientist, given over to a drive and a power that was beyond himself, that did not care for the body of the man it inhabited nor the planet in the making, sought to challenge the command. It was a force in rebellion, a power that moved and had at its centre an impulse that drew to destruction and disorder. The pressure on the woman was unremitting. The pull towards chaos and a disobedience to the inner voice that kept all in harmony, went on and on and on. A battle was fought, without banners or drums. Two middle-aged men holding each other in deadly embrace, fought, skin stuck to skin, the nerves pricking and trembling with exhaustion. At the centre of the struggle the will to corrupt or preserve flickered and flared. A voice in the darkness that followed after in the long exhausted night, spoke to a man called Ransom. He learnt his name was not without significance.

I know now that all the most important battles are on the inside. It is from within our minds that the battle lines are fought. It is within the mind that the enemy is identified as the outsider. If we but knew, the enemy is within our skin. Wars and rumours of wars begin with a word and a thought, with fear of a threat; with an idea, and for a word and a name, lives are lost and lands are gained.

. . . I see
the imminent death of twenty thousand men,
That for a fantasy and trick of fame,
go to their graves like beds; fight for a plot
Whereon the numbers cannot try the cause,
Which is not tomb enough and continent
To hide the slain?' (*Hamlet* Act 4 Scene 5)

In my hospital bed, so alone in my particular darkness, I had begun a battle that intermittently rages still. I wondered then, whether any voice, within or without, would speak to me, to tell me that my life also mattered, and although I was one amongst the million millions, I had a place, a part to play in the pattern of things.

What I did not know then, was that if the Voice did

speak, that speaking would pose as many problems as it might solve. Nothing is beyond doubt, and I was born and reared in an age of reason and a time whose god is Science. My training has not given me many tools for dealing with and distinguishing the Divine Other. Nothing is beyond doubt. Hamlet was right to say to his friend Horatio, trained like himself in the sceptical Wittenberg University, that, 'There's more in heaven and earth, Horatio, than is dreamed of in your philosophy.' But my, oh my, when the ghost you do not believe in walks on your inner stage, it takes quite a lot to get over the shock, never mind begin to muster up the courage actually to deal with the message. I have a lot of sympathy for Hamlet nowadays.

My mother, not realising the hand grenades she was carrying home with her in her shopping basket, combed the local library to pick out for me choice specimens that would be hidden round the house: behind jars of coffee and tins of cakes in the pantry, underneath or behind coats in a cupboard.

Seeing the restlessness in the eyes and body of her daughter, I would be banished from the maternal presence and a book would be spirited from its hiding place amongst the pots and pans, to be triumphantly displayed to the tired, bored eyes, which for once, obedient enough, came when called back.

The visions within the minds of Henry Treece, C. S. Lewis and Rosemary Sutcliff stalked through my head and changed the colour of the world within.

I understand now why the heretic-hunter and the Secret Police of all the tyrannies in the world, fear the power of the word, whether printed or on the lips of living people.

Alone, whilst my mother worked through the long summer break, I ferreted around in the kitchen and the pantry, hoping against hope to find some hidden treasure. At last it came. Like a ferret nosing its prey, the nose for the book found it out, in a most unlikely hiding place . . . inside the washing machine!

It was the last of the Narnian stories, *The Last Battle*. Curled in the corner of myself and in the large and capacious embrace of the old, brown sofa, which could even accommodate the white elephantine legs, I read and read and read. I wasn't quite the same human being when I had finished. I don't think I have ever been quite the same again . . . and that was only the first merest hint and whisper of a beginning, a trumpet's cry from a far distance. But I hear it and hear it still—the call that sounds in a particular quality of silence.

In this story, Aslan, the Great Lion, who had kept absence when his world was dying and in its last death agonies, came back at last to the world that he had made . . .

Oh, the pain of the absence of God when the night is at its blackest, yet the glory that comes after is commensurate with the weight of the pain that went before . . . if we will but wait. I never knew till now the challenge and the strength required for the positive power of waiting . . . of waiting for the light to return after the night. All nights have their mornings. They are inextricably bound together. All endings are also beginnings and all beginnings are also endings; it was always so.

In the context of the world of the other, I listened in to a Lion, of gold and living, breathing majesty . . . a golden wonder of gentle strength, explaining to the children who had held true to a Truth that they had known as living beings, even when all the lights had gone out . . . and who had seen the last battle fought—the battle that was on the inside as well as without—that that Truth had come for them as they had hoped. When they thought that the wonder and the pain and the mystery were to be ended, they found it had only begun . . . because, as Aslan explained:

'"You are as you used to call it in the shadowlands—dead. The term is over; the holidays have begun. The dream is ended; this is the morning . . ." And as He spoke He no longer looked to them like a lion . . . and for us this is the end of all stories. But for them it was only the beginning of the real story. All their life in this world and all their adventures in Narnia, had only been the cover and title page; now at last they were beginning chapter one of the Great story in which every chapter is better than the one before . . .'

My heart leapt, with a wild hope and a beginning of a sense that perhaps this was not just a story . . . that this just might be a glimpse of a truth of how it was . . . of how it is. I closed the book but did not move. A silence within and in the outer air held me still. The quiet crept on unbroken. No voice was heard in that suburban house by that Jewish child, not yet, for the time wasn't ready, nor would I have been able to bear it.

With an effort both physical and emotional, I prized myself and my boots out of the armchair to get my father's lunch.

He was in bed again, staring at the ceiling, alone in the locked bedroom. What did he see in ceilings? They did not have much to recommend them, in my opinion. Boring, ceilings were, with only the odd wandering crack or two to repay any interest at all. With some effort, if you had to, you could transform a ceiling into a map of an undiscovered land . . . and trace out the contours of new islands, new continents of magic and danger, round the wandering of the cracks and the gaps in the plastering, but really ceilings were most monotonous as far as detailed study was concerned. I really could not understand why my father paid them so much attention. What made a father sleep and sleep the days and weeks away . . . sleep away the love and care of his wife and children?

What was he trying to forget? What did he not want to know? He had given up the battle, leaving his wife to struggle on to earn the bread for the little ones, now nearly full grown. He had given up the battle in the outside world; thrown in the towel, telling the umpire not to ring the bell for any more rounds for him. But the shadows in the mind are not so obedient. They fight on and on, round and round the circle of the brain until finding courage from somewhere, we turn and face what we do not want, and in that upturning and in that facing, we find that the lions are chained on each side of the path. As we turn and walk towards them, they grow smaller and smaller until we pass through the centre. The path goes inbetween, leading us beyond the roar and menace of what had imprisoned us for so long on this side of fear.

So I was alone in the house with my sleeping father. My mother away at the shop that we all hated, because it was a way of life not chosen. The psychiatrist had suggested it as a way of relieving the tension my father experienced in having to work for another's pleasure at another's command. I wish psychiatrists listened to the mothers and sisters and children caught in the circle of pain. We could have told him what would happen if, as he had suggested, we took over when my father couldn't cope. 'You can carry on for him' he had said. Necessity can be a great teacher, albeit an uncomfortable one. There are times when we need the lessons of necessity and it is no kindness to remove the pressure it puts upon us. We could have told him, my brother, mother and I . . . We could have said but we didn't. We knew what would happen and it did . . .

In a matter of months my mother was 'carrying on' for him . . . of course. Desperate, tired and despairing, she kept the place going, helped now by my brother, who had left school early to help lighten the weary task. Someone had to keep going. Mother and son toiled amongst sweet jars and boxes of chocolate delights.

Father and daughter at a different task. The one encased and cocooned in blankets against a cold and a darkness that could not be measured by thermometer or meter-gauge . . . and the daughter hidden behind the shield-ring of the printed page—my last defence against the silent howling of the wolf in winter behind the locked doors.

My father was the original gourmand of sleep if quantity was anything to go by. I did not know then what I know now . . .

'No worst, there is none. Pitched past pitch of grief,
More pangs will, schooled at forepangs, wilder wring.
Comforter, where, where is your comforting?
Mary mother of us, where is your relief?
My cries heave, herds-long; huddle in a main, a chief
Woe, world-sorrow; on an age-old anvil wince and sing—
Then lull, then leave off. Fury had shrieked 'No lingering!
Let me be fell: force I must be brief.

O the mind, mind has mountains; cliffs of fall
Frightful, sheer, no-man-fathomed. Hold them cheap
May who ne'er hung there. Nor does long our small
Durance deal with that steep or deep. Here! creep,
Wretch, under a comfort serves in a whirlwind: all
Life death does end and each day dies with sleep.'

(Gerard Manley Hopkins Sonnet 42.)

So my father lay incarcerated amongst the blankets, staring at the ceiling . . . his sleep aided and abetted by the myriad, multi-coloured pills that arrayed the mantlepiece—chemical rainbows of an illusionary hope; pretty pills that did not sweeten but only deadened life.

What did he think of as hour after hour staggered by unremarked, unsung, a stream that passed him by? I do not know, but I did know that it did not improve his temper.

The homely fragrance of scrambled egg and beans on toast must have tiptoed round the locked door, to tempt my father to a reappearance in the land of the living. I had made a somewhat pathetic attempt to create an air of normality and order on the breakfast room table. The clean cloth proudly sported the cutlery; tea-pot and plates carefully arranged. Lunch for two. Well it looked quite cosy and inviting . . . not for long though.

I can't remember what acted as the catalyst. I remember no word, just a look. The snarling curled lip of a wolf, an angry wolf; a wolf in winter who was starving but who could not eat.

The tablecloth complete with contents desperately and unsuccessfully trying to balance on their white magic carpet, was torn from its resting place and flung, along with its residents, in a shower of broken fragments that bounced off door and walls. Boiling tea became a shower of painful rain that burnt the skin. The table crashed in protest onto its side with a groan. I grovelled at its feet, bending my head to hide the scalding shame of tears of fright and anger and shock. Sodden tea-leaves trailed across the carpet, in thick, brown, sinuous curves. Butter was splattered across the chairlegs, wallpaper and floor, along with the glorious mess of egg, beans and bits of toast.

What had I done wrong? I do not know. Nothing, I think.

A volcano had erupted. The door slammed upstairs, the lock a pistol shot. The house returned to its quiet and its waiting.

I stopped the tears. What was the use of tears? They did no good. They solved nothing. They did not clear up the mess. It has taken many years before I have let myself cry again. Slowly, slowly I have learnt that to stop up grief is to create a worse mess than the mess of eggs and beans and tea, besmirching the walls and floor.

Laboriously I got to the phone, squelching yet more tea-leaves underfoot.

Brr. Brr. Brr. Brr.

'Mum, Mum are you there? I don't know what to do. Dad's thrown the table over—food's all over the floor . . . and my arm's burnt . . . and the room's in a terrible mess. What? No . . . I don't think the arm's serious, but it's scalded a bit I think . . . Mum I'm frightened . . . No, I'm not hungry. No, I don't want anything. Yes, I'll come right away . . . I'll manage . . . I've got your stick . . .'

Another door slammed. It was all the protest I could make. The wood groaned with the force of the blow, poor thing. Old-woman-like I heaved and squeaked my way down the path to the bus, leaving my father behind me, with his thoughts and his pills in an emptied house.

The summer dragged itself along, day by leaden day. My back pricked with tension, tight with unspoken questions and uncertainty.

One day we returned from the hated shop, where my brother was carefully and patiently trying to create some semblance of business-like order, from all of his sixteen years, and where I had sat all day hunched, crumpled and cold over a tiny Belling stove, resentfully trying to read and to forget the smutty, grubby, little boys who came in for yet another 'gob-stopper'. On the dark brown Jacobean oak of the settle-seat in the hall, usually the place for the flung-down school bag and detested uniform grey-gaberdine, was a note. A stiff, white, upright note. On best Basildon Bond, it was. The pristine white of the envelope was propped proudly erect, awaiting our coming in. It was a note not to be missed. It was like a soldier note—a message from the War Office, but there was no official stamp. But we knew . . . without reading it we knew.

My stomach did a backward flip and then curled hard and round like a fist: a fist that made me feel sick. The fist closed my throat but my foot was on the stair, ready to run, to phone the doctor, the ambulance . . . Quick! Quick! . . . We must do something quickly . . .

'Let's put a record on,' said my brother. His face was impassive; the voice calm.

The fist in my throat dropped away in amazement.

But . . . but shouldn't we *do* something . . . I mean . . . we must . . . He's, he's . . . surely . . . the note . . . we must do something . . .'

'He's dead, isn't he? So there is nothing to be done. He's dead . . . that's what he says . . .' The note was now in my big brother's hand. 'Well, if he's dead he can't hear then, can he? So there is nothing we can do then, is there?'

My brother's face was set . . . calm. The stiffness of the paper on which the note had been written had been transferred into a stiffness of bone and skin and muscle.

I followed at his heels, stunned. He put a record on, my brother did. Now the stiffness was sent away as his long, lean, near-young-man's body lounged against the cushions in the faded Parker-Knoll armchair. It was a good mimicry, the body entering with a will into the spirit of the game. But what game was it we played? In heaven and earth, what game was being played out that day?

The record was put on. I can't remember what it was. But I remember that it was loud, very, very loud. Music filled the room. Bursting from its prison, it spread through door and ceiling—a cry of defiance against the suicide note, against the shut bedroom door, the comatose, thick, slumped body amidst the bedraggled bedclothes.

On the edge of the chair I waited, listening, appalled.

I knew the meaning of the music blaring and was glad, glad that my brother was fighting back. I realised that the protest might get through, battering by sheer volume through the thick-drugged sleep . . . and what then? We sat on, surrounded by sound . . . waiting.

But nothing happened.

The next day assumed again a normal shape. My father eventually woke up. The note was gone.

Nothing was said.

Chapter 7

'Why is this night different from all other nights?' says the youngest child at the Passover feast. There were nights like that in our house, but the question was never asked and there was no feast, but only a silence to ask it of. What went before I never knew, not until the last night. That night ended the nights that were different from other nights. It sounds such a little thing—in comparison to the horrors and cruelties that some endure, such a little, little thing. But little things can be a clue, a sign that not all is well, not all is right. A little thing can tip a balance so that until the right order is restored we live askew. It's fairly uncomfortable living askew. I know. I've tried it.

So what made some nights different? Just a little thing . . . a noise . . . a shape, the bulk of my father lifting my sleep-drugged body. When I woke I was not in my little bed, under the window in my room, my haven, where the cold winds did not blow, or so I thought. I was in my parents' bedroom in my father's bed wondering how the world had come so puzzlingly to reorganise itself. Why was I here and my room locked against me? Even the night could not be trusted.

Nothing was said.

'Dad, Dad, can't I come in now?'

'Go away!'

I went away, a stray dog. I didn't belong in my mother's bedroom. I didn't feel right. It wasn't my place. My mother's silence made my head ache. We both pretended that all was well. It seemed the easier way and life was quite hard enough, thank you.

Now I know that the easier way usually turns out the hardest in the end. The longest and slowest way up the mountain may be the one to get you to the top, with even the odd beautiful and majestic view to catch your breath and strengthen your spirit along the way. The wide and nettle-free path, in my experience, often seems to land me in a ditch or looking wearily at a chasm that I cannot cross: the only way up then being a slow and even more laborious going-back to the path I had so faint-heartedly spurned, nettles and all.

I hate nettles.

So my mother and I said nothing. There was quite a lot of 'nothing' about in our house. Or rather it was an absence of certain words. It's amazing what power absence has. So we both pretended that all was well, that somehow this was quite a normal state of affairs. There was nowhere to go, nowhere to hide, so I stayed where I was: out of place, not at home in my home.

A day came and went . . . a night and another night passed, the warm dark eventually sending my rigid child's body into sleep. Then as unexpectedly as I had arrived in my mother's room, one morning I was back in my own. Back in the bed by the window, listening to the rain mutter on the roof.

Were other fathers like this? Were other children removed from their beds at dead of night and left with their mothers? Why wasn't my brother disturbed? Why was it always me? What made my father leave his room so late in the night? Why did he lock us away, barricading himself in with lock and bolt against a woman and two children? What harm could we do?

My brother and I joined in an alliance, a confederacy

against the cold that crept into our eyes as we watched the winter wolf, starving and angry, brooding over the carefully prepared meal. My mother bent her head, her eyes gazing fixedly at the shiny glaze. But the pretty patterns of the plate did not answer her.

'What's this bloody muck?'

My mother's voice was quiet, gentle, weary and resigned; a no-hope voice.

'Barley stew. You always used to say it was your favourite . . .'

'Sue,' my brother's voice nudged me out of my misery, as his foot poked mine under the table. His voice dropped to a conspiratorial whisper . . . 'I think the outlook for the weather this evening is becoming cloudy. Storms are gathering on the horizon and the temperature . . . the temperature . . .'

My brother paused and glanced with an inquiring lift of an arched eyebrow at my father's scowling face and then with a knowing look at my strained face . . . 'Yes, . . . the er . . . temperature is dropping steadily . . . it might reach zero freezing point before long . . .'

Before the drop in pressure and temperature froze us, we had the quick, statutory row between brother and sister as to who should wash up, some normality remaining even as the 'weather' cooled. As the cold increased our smiles froze and we ran—ran from the atmosphere that could be cut like a cake, but unlike my mother's cakes it didn't taste good.

Where did I run to? I had a haven. There is usually somewhere waiting for us: a special place we bump into, that finds us as much as we find it. My haven wasn't anything special. It suited me . . . a piece of sliding water and an iron bridge. Over the months and years I perfected the art of sitting rather precariously balanced, propped up by an iron balustrade, still seated on the bike, watching the slow, meandering of the weary but patient water. The constant quiet movement with its sliding circles eased away the iron band around my head. It wasn't really beautiful or clean, that bit of Mersey tucked away at the back of houses in a crowded city, but it was a haven still, a smelly haven, but itself and kind.

* * *

To be ill, well, not too ill, could be rather fun. The cosy bed, the night-light, the extra fruit and time off school were treats that made sickness at times preferable to health.

But not all sickness was so nice. There were times when my heart pumped and pushed like a worn-out steam traction engine, my lungs gurgling and groaning in a vain struggle to get breath. Then the doctor would come and a needle would make my breath thud, thud in my veins like a greyhound suddenly let out on the track racing to a far horizon. It was frightening but it helped . . . until the next time.

I remember my brother's gentle gifts, his thoughtful eyes; my mother's quiet care; the relief of the bowl of steaming water with its hot face-flannel, wiping away the sticky sweat; the cool calm of the newly-stretched sheets, coaxed into order from the chaos of wrinkles and rumples. But most of all I remember being lulled into the sleep that would not come for me, no matter how much I entreated, but that came to the bidding of my mother, whose hand on her daughter's hot forehead beat a slow steady rhythm that pushed the restlessness away beyond the room. Breathing was no longer the same struggle. With the help of that hand, sleep came.

How can you ease the pain of the soul and calm its frightened breathing? We did not know, my family and I. We needed to know. In that need and from that not-knowing has begun a search that has shaped my life, even as the shadows of the past shaped and patterned the choices and the experience of my father.

A different sickness grew and began to take shape.

The bulk of my father shadowed and blocked the doorway.

He did not move out of or into the room but stood transfixed between the two. He looked at me with a strange expression on his face.

'Sue, your father . . .' (why did he say 'your father' and not 'I'?) 'Your father's not really well. I'm going for a short sort of holiday in Scotland for a couple of weeks . . .'

He waited and needed some certain reply.

The solid shadow in the doorway was fixed, as if rooted like a tree: a solidity in space; a solidity around a space at the centre. At the centre he was cold, my father . . . too cold. His bulk did not move from between the lintels of the door.

And so a man looked at a young girl: his daughter. What did he see? What did he want? I can guess now. He waited for hope . . . for a little compassion from the girl who was his and yet not his . . . from the girl who was not yet woman. But then I was unaware: innocent, ignorant and unaware, shut off by my own pain, by my youth, by fear and the silence.

Where was he going? What did he mean? What could I say?

I examined these assorted questions. They sat and stared back at me from the kitchen linoleum. I hoped for inspiration. It did not come.

'How long will you be away?'

'A week, two weeks, perhaps more . . .'

The words grew sick themselves and wobbled to a stop. I longed to say . . . 'But Dad, you aren't ill . . . You're not sick or pale; you've not bones broken, no wounds, no raw flesh to make you wince and ache . . .'

I didn't realise then, being too new to living, that you could be nailed through the mind by a face, by a mother's face; a face that never smiled. I didn't know then that that face could so freeze his mind and heat his blood, that he longed to hurt and hurt as he'd been hurt, to lash out and wound another woman's face . . . and my mother was a woman . . .

I stared at my feet in silence; the words having wandered away and my questions with them.

I looked up: the kitchen was empty.

Chapter 8

I didn't realise for many years how many different forms silence takes. There are currents and tidal waves in aloneness. In the silence the tide comes in or goes out. We do well to know the current, to estimate its strength and force before venturing out for a swim. I wonder sometimes if there is an ebb and flow of the tide in the affairs of the nations: the nations being a macrocosm of the microcosm that is the life of one person. Looking backwards and forwards across the line of time, it looks so, history showing the fall of dynasties and the rise of new powers. But what is behind the rise and the fall? The affairs of the nations are, after all, the affairs of people. Nothing just happens.

Jung was right when he said that the second half of life was taken up with the questions. In the second half of my life it is the meaning of things that dominate the inner landscape. Mind you, that particular question cropped up for me many, many years ago: a sharp and jagged rock; a great mountain jutting out of the hot stifled air that blew in the desert of the silences, that echoes from the room with the locked door where my father slept.

I remember asking that question in the outer world for the first time. When the words had given it shape and form, the shadow it cast made me cold—but I think I was cold already.

A year had passed. A slow, slow, weary year, full of plodding, painful days and listening nights. A mother sat with a daughter nearly grown at her knee. Somehow, in the quiet that tugged at me on starlit nights, the question that stood with me on the landing outside that frowning door—the question that spoke in the silence beneath the grey, swirling mass of clouds and rain in the storms I so loved, spoke itself. In one form or another it will be asked by all of us—there is no escaping. One day we look it straight in the face and find our way to an answer or die. I have known some who have died for want of an answer: for want of the 'Golden City'.

Ten little girls from school are we,
plaited, pony-tailed, socks to the knee.
Some are as smart as smart can be,
and each one of us is pretty.

Rosie Fagan says she'll cry
if she doesn't get the fellow with the roving eye.
Elsie Geraghty says she'll die
for want of the Golden City.

The wind, the wind, the wind blows high
the rain comes tumbling from the sky

some are bound to travel far,
go through the world like a shooting star.
Some will shunt like an old street car.

some will fall right over the edge
to the place where all the nightmares lodge.
Some will always cling to a ledge.

The wind, the wind, the wind blows high
the snow comes drifting from the sky

Some get pudding and still want pie.
Some settle for a fellow with a roving eye,
and some will pine and some will die
for want of the Golden City.

(Evangeline Patterson)

And so the question spoke itself.

'Mother . . . do you believe in God? A real God, not a Force . . . or a blind and unknowing stream . . . but a God . . . a Being who is personal, who cares whether we live or die. Do you, Mum? Is there anything, somewhere . . . something?'

The mother stared into space, her fingers blindly stroking the hair of the daughter. Round and round the fingers went, making a curl of the wild, untidy, so undemure hair. The silence began to stretch itself, tightening its length. The minutes ticked themselves past. The daughter confided to the floral carpet that if there were Nothing, there seemed no point in living at all. It would be like the Roman slave before the arena, 'Eat, drink, sleep and be merry, for tomorrow we die'.

I ask that question still.

I begin to have a few hints and shadows of a response—an answer that is not in words, that is contained in part within words but points always beyond them . . . outward and upwards and inwards and beyond . . . always beyond. There is that hint of a pattern, that whisper that there *is* meaning, that the living out of a small life in all its complexities and simplicities matters. It matters beyond matter. How or why I'm not too sure. There are pointers, clues and signposts. I'm on my way, I think. Nothing is as certain as I once thought in my past innocence and youth. But perhaps it is all more certain than we know: 'Now we see as in a glass, darkly; then we shall see face to face . . . and know as we are known . . .' What a statement! It quite takes my breath away. One day I might get used to it. Twenty odd years after I first read it, it still nearly flattens me with the immensity of its claim.

Nothing was said.

The daughter went on, 'You see . . . if there's Nothing, then it's all a meaningless jangle . . . absurd. Nothing matters. It doesn't matter what we do.'

The silence lengthened further and wound itself towards the door. Tracing the pattern of the stylised flowers and fern, I waited hungrily for an answer that would ease the fear of vast wastes of nothingness, my life a speck of dust in an infinity of space and howling emptiness.

The lounge was now packed and thick with the absence of words. I looked up at my mother's face. It was wet with tears.

'I don't know . . . perhaps the rabbi? I don't know. I don't know how to help you. I just don't know . . . you can't know . . .'

But if there was . . . you could.

* * *

I had prayed for the first time six months before, or rather attempted to pray. It's an odd experience. Quite uncomfortable really, like talking into the receiver of a telephone after you have just catapulted down the stairs, after having heard it ringing. Then on picking up the insistent thing . . . silence. Idiotically, you ask of the silence, 'Is anybody there?' Silence . . . and then a click.

My first prayer felt like that. Except—had the phone rung? But maybe a crisis is the ringing of the bell. I didn't say, 'Is anyone there?' but I certainly thought it. It was a prayer typical of many such beginnings, but none the worse for that. What was it, the stumbling start? Just, 'God . . . Oh God help us!' More like a gasp of pain than a prayer, but perhaps the two are not so dissimilar.

I did not know whether anyone heard or listened, there in the quiet dark of our Blackpool hotel.

I heard no answer.

I did not know what help I would have liked, nor whether I would have recognised it had it come. I'd have wished one could find a magic wand to wave to make it all better, to make the mess go away, but of course there was none to be had. (None that I could see anyway, tucked away amongst the shell ornaments and the slightly fluorescent shocking pink rock.)

Why were we there for this sudden 'holiday'? Nothing had been said but deep down at the bottom I knew. Perhaps one always does.

'Sue, I've been thinking . . .' The tired lines in my mother's too-soon-old face sank a bit deeper with the sigh.

The sentence was never finished. I finished it for her, with longing, with hope, with relief.

'Are we going then? Are you going to leave?'

I half wanted her to ask me how I felt. My tone was uncharacteristically restrained. If I'd been asked, hot words of hurt would have hurried out, blood spurting from a wound, but the question was never asked and so they stayed where they were, hidden, black words that would blacken my sight for a while.

Neither of us spoke. We both listened. The oath of the traditional wedding service rang in our ears: 'In sickness and health, until death us do part . . .'

Behind the sick tiredness of her eyes, my mother was balancing the lives of three against the life of the one.

Little did I think that my time would come, when I also would listen to that oath in a silent room and in that silence twenty years on, would hear a Voice, a voice that spoke across the boundaries of the inner and outer worlds; a voice such as I had read about. And in that speaking and in that listening I was changed and my understanding of the moral law: the law that was sacred and weighty and holy, the Law that was a part of my race, a part of my history and a part of my blood, was altered, never to be the same again.

But this was then . . . not now—yet in that 'then' was the 'now'—there are times when the sense of a returning and the working out of a pattern frightens me. I am not made of sterling stuff; more like sawdust and feathers and bits of fluff; apple cores and peach stones and all manner of stuff . . .

My mother's tired voice went on . . . 'Your father and I . . . you see . . . I . . . I think that it might be a good idea if your father and I lived apart for a while. I've left a note for your father, saying we've gone away for a short holiday . . . that I'm going to think things over. He doesn't know where we are. Don't worry. Shall we go down to dinner now?'

My mother put on her face: a smiling, gracious surface from her handbag, along with the powder on her nose.

The daughter went ahead, pretending—for a moment the grown-up veneer slipped aside—that she was a lift attendant. The mother followed sedately down the stairs.

My mother didn't like lifts. I always found the closing click of the lift-gates very satisfying. I wonder why. Was it a shutting out or a shutting in that I heard in that 'click'. And what was shut in or out?

I turned round to look for my mother coming down the re-carpeted stairs of this North Beach Hotel. My face went very, very cold—so cold it shivered.

'Well, aren't you going to say hello to your poor old father?'

We needed no Gorgon, my mother and I. We were turned to stone and stood transfixed amongst the gilt and red plush.

What on earth would happen now?

Now it was I who tried to rearrange my face . . . unsuccessfully. I've got better at it since, when I choose. I'm not sure whether it's always wise, but without a doubt it's useful at times, the rearrangement of the face. I get better at it by turns.

The truth can be a very cold wind. It can burn your face and hands and heart. A bare face is not always a good idea in a blizzard.

Chapter 9

Three's an awkward number, yet at times it can be a power: creative, a divine, not an infernal triangle. This three was awkward all right. I don't really know why I was there, sitting staring fixedly at my feet in the back of the car. I had no place in this conversation. This talking was for husband and wife; it was between man and woman. This was grown-up talk, not for children.

Yet I was not exactly a child and the talk was about what I knew; it was about what would affect my life. So I was there and yet not there; a bystander, a spectator at a man's desperate attempt to save the final dying of his marriage, his family and his home.

'Too late! Too late!' I wanted to cry through the streets and byways of his mind; a Cassandra crying in the night. But the cry remained enclosed in my bones, heard only by my racing blood.

Desperation can galvanise talent and energy in a most concentrated form. My father talked with passion, fluency, intensity and a conviction I had never heard before or since. I can only remember a few of the words that poured out of him. They look so sad now, battered and tattered remnants of flags that blew bravely in the wind of his hope, for such a brief, brief moment.

'I won't bother you . . . I have a plan . . . I'll go and live at the shop. You will have time and space and I will only come when you ask. I love you. Hannah, I love you. I've only ever loved you. I want you back. You're everything to me. You and the children . . . my home. Give me a chance. We'll sort the money out somehow. I'm sure that that's the biggest of the problems, what is worrying you the most. If we can get that off your mind, the rest will follow . . . Give me six months . . . just six months. Just a few months. You wouldn't deny me that . . . surely . . .'

Inside my face I was a Goneril and a Regan. A face of flint stared at my summer-sandalled feet. I listened to my mother's silence and my father's torrent of words. I knew she would say yes . . . that she could not resist that torrent, not for long. I suppose you always hope.

To have lived together with a man for twenty odd years, your body having been altered by his; grown big with his children's bodies. Together to have seen your children grow. Such bonds of blood and memory are not easily broken. This I know from the inside now. Then I did not know, but guessed . . . a little.

Perhaps this time he might change. Perhaps this time her actual going might concentrate his mind, make him seek new ways . . . Perhaps this time it might be better and he would understand that she could not just go on and on and on, no matter what he was like or what he did . . . that she needed something too. Perhaps this time he could see that loving and commitment and loyalty and the marriage vow could not go on unaided . . . that it took two . . .

What did she think, my mother? I do not know. I can only guess. So little was said.

I remember my mother's few, quiet words trailing off as if as tired and ill as the body that uttered them, until they flopped to a halt on the windscreen. I can't remember the words but I remember the sense of the quiet, weary, voice. 'Well, perhaps. We'll give it a last try . . . for six months . . .'

In my flint-like mood I didn't even bother to snort my

disgust and disbelief. Six months, was it? It lasted a week, I think. Maybe a little more. Then he was back, my father . . . the same as ever . . . of course.

There were a couple more suicide attempts and a few more months packed with anger and blood-flecked words. Then the violence and self-hatred in my father moved outwards.

Unknown to me at the time, my mother twice struggled for her life. If he was going to go, he would take her with him; the two were to be found dead in a gas-filled, suburban-lounge room: everything neat and tidy and homely, only the two bodies and the smell denoting the poison that had turned life against itself. That night my mother fought as she had never fought before. My mother is not used to fighting. She felt then that she was given a strength: a strength from beyond her and yet within her, a strength she had not known. Another night would come when she would fight again, fight for the life of herself and her children. That night now was on its way to our door. The policemen were its heralds.

We were not a family that had much dealing with the police. We were respectable and law-abiding and policemen were our friends, or so we thought, my brother and I. The dreadful things you read about in the papers did not happen to us. *Scream Quietly or the Neighbours will Hear* had not yet been written, but such things were not to do with us. We were not like that. We were not those sort of people. Or so we thought. Well, you live and learn and life is full of surprises . . . not always pleasant ones.

So how did it begin—our respectable, unrespectable involvement with a struggle that would call the police to our door? Or, rather more accurately, would make my fingers, cold and slippy with fear, dial the 999 that I had thought I would never ring.

Well . . . I said that three can be an awkward number.

This time it was mother and father and son. Perhaps it wasn't a three but rather a two; an alliance that was known and sensed long before but took years to come to its maturity. Who knows? Only the three who took part. I was the bystander, watching: terrified, horrified, helpless.

*   *   *

Most times I was really glad I had a brother; big brother, freckle-faced with ears that stuck out from his head, fellow-hater of games. I followed faithfully in his footsteps, or rather at the rear of his bicycle wheels! Big brother, who was so tall and so thin and ate so many potatoes: twelve once, at one sitting—and no one ever called him greedy! Brother with red hair and thin, knobbly knees and a slow smile that eased its way reluctantly across his face, spreading round his beaked nose and up into quiet eyes.

Brother: my mother's son . . .

I would hear my mother laughing. Coming into the room I expected the telling of a joke or funny story . . . but no . . .

'Mum . . . Mum . . . what are you laughing at?'

'Oh just your brother's expression. He's got such a funny expression!'

I would squint in an effort to work out what was so funny about it. It looked quite normal to me. Two eyes, two ears, eagle nose and his usual pursed mouth. No matter how hard I concentrated it looked quite normal . . . a face both like and unlike others, as was my own. My mother never laughed that way with me. Mind you, I can't blame her really; not much to laugh at, serious-plump-pudding that I was, with my nose for ever in a book. Still, it was strange how much my brother and mother would laugh together. Slowly I realised that she was laughing with him. Mother and son would laugh at I knew not what. They were an alliance against the world; an alliance against the shadow that enclosed me and my father; an alliance that sometimes, through the vehicle of jokes and teases, turned against me: mother and son, laughing at this over-solemn, so serious, fat little girl. I am sure there was much to laugh about. But oh, how I hated it! I hated and fought against it with shouts and shrieks and childish, blushing, impotent rage. The two, so unaware, could not understand the hot, dark anger of the little girl who could not bear to lose, who verbally kicked and kicked against the laughter: the laughter that shut her out.

For the alliance that I was drawn into with my father, I did not want. I had nowhere to go; if these two were not for me, what hope was there?

He drew me to his side, my father did. After play or film it was always me that he had to walk with. It was the daughter he wanted as a talisman against the dark that would always follow like the night the day. Cocooned in its shadow we walked the hard, grey concrete home, my mother and brother following at a safe distance, free for a while. So I was left to be Daddy's girl. I did not want it. I did not choose it. But then I had no power to make it different: to change the pattern that was spun for me. Such webs take years to make. They may take years to break.

So father and daughter were separated from mother and son.

Down the years I hear my mother's laughter, gay as a girl, with my brother. Did she laugh with my father so when they were young? I do not know, but I think perhaps they did. I hope that my father and his wife had such laughter. It's part of what's special between the man and the woman who choose each other. Was it the dying of the laughter that fuelled the fire that brought the police to our door? Was it hearing that laughter that was not for him, that was not with him, that turned father against son? Mind you it was years and years since my father laughed. Indeed I never remember it. There was not a lot of laughter in our house. What killed the capacity for laughter in my father? What destroyed the laughter in the mother who bore this son? I will never know.

What I did know was that this talent of my brother's for making my mother laugh was annoying. His ability to make my mother collapse into girlish giggles was distinctly useful: like when the special Lalique plate was broken, or a sparkler had been swung too near the wooden box that kept our cutlery. The parental fury was allayed, quickly, effectively and permanently by this same talent. You cannot be angry with the son you are laughing at and with. It really was a most functional and useful talent. Life was so unjust.

But I was still happy that I had a brother. I was not alone in the storms that blew. Sometimes we made our own alliance and it made me feel a little warmer.

During one long bout of illness I remember my brother furtively hiding a small package and a book in a bottom drawer, whilst I was supposed to be asleep. I could hardly wait for the door to close quietly. I cheated and tiptoed guiltily, choc-a-bloc full of curiosity to find what those alluring parcels were. I never was a patient child.

I will never forget his quiet care and thoughtful sensitivity in those carefully chosen presents, for a hot and restless, confined-to-bed sister. I can see them now . . . a little purse, pretty plastic with a gold-bobbly-necklace-type handle, and the first book I remember reading on my own, *Black Beauty.* Little things can have great moment. Little things can make or break. It is in the little things that we are prepared. Only fools plunge into the deep end first before they've learnt to swim.

Words can make or break too. Although what Malcolm says to Macduff in *Macbeth* is, I believe, profoundly true, as any psychiatrist will tell you, that it is a wise thing to: '. . . speak your grief/Give sorry words: the grief that does not speak/Whispers the o'er-fraught heart, and bids it break.' But words can have great negative force too. They are powers we use often unawares.

My brother had had enough of these words: of the curses that hurled themselves with such fury through the air at my silent mother as we sat at the meal table. This time he hurled something back: a challenge; a defiance; a protection for my mother, hunched silent and terrified as old and young dog growled and snapped—the one loud, the other dangerously controlled.

Two women looked on at an age-old drama.

Glass and pottery turned to weapons and then brother and son, husband and father, were locked in deadly embrace, squirming and twisting on the carpeted stairs, hands clutching and clawing for a hold around the throat.

Then the siren outside the door, the flash of the blue light, swirling in the dark outside the panes of the stained-glass panels in the front door.

My hands had developed a life of their own. Round and round they went as if washing themselves like Lady Macbeth's. Round and round in a frantic circle, as I begged the two silently striving men, turning and twisting on the stairway, 'Stop! Please, please stop!'

It's amazing how the habit of politeness sticks with you. I can't say it was really appropriate to the moment looking back. But the police would *do* something. That's what they were for, wasn't it, to stop people getting hurt or hurting others. Well, I'd got the general message right, only there was one rather important exclusion clause, that no doubt is in some small print still in a Police manual somewhere . . .

The door was open, the dark uniformed figures stood on the doorstep and saw behind the terrified women, the two men, heaving and straining on the stairs, oblivious of the strangers on the threshold.

'Please, please make them stop. Stop them!' I cried and

pleaded, expecting them to wade in and separate the fighting men and the danger with it.

The impassive uniformed figures made words that I heard in the air. I could not believe them.

'Sorry Missus, we can't do anything if it's a family dispute.'

I wanted to rage and shout, to run into the street screaming, shouting down curses on the Law that did not protect me or my mother or brother from a raging father. If we were dead perhaps then they might do something. If they saw us askew and covered with blood—after the event—then perhaps the Law might step in and take some note . . . but now . . . Oh no! Within the home the father was king. We were left to it: the Panda car taking itself and its blue light with it.

We were lucky. There were no bloody remains for the police to come for that night. The momentum had been stopped. The fighting men had heard the siren and the official voices. We were lucky; the blue bystanders, the strangers on the threshold, had broken the spell. It was over.

So we staggered on for a month or two. At school I studied for O-levels, trying to apply my mind to French verbs, physics definitions and a Shakespeare text. Life went on in a fashion. Each night I did not know what the evening would bring. We were in the phoney war. All seemed calm but war had been declared. Normality such as I knew could not last much longer. I was right. It didn't.

They say life's stranger than fiction. It is.

* * *

Images from another night that was not like any other night are frozen like stills from the video recorder. Barricaded into the bedroom frantically helping my brother haul the wardrobe and chairs against the door; barricaded against a father raging through a suburban semi, knife in hand; the crashing of the glass of the French windows in the room below us; my body hanging like a soggy mattress over the window sill; a voice that was mine yelling for help and, even as I did so, feeling an idiot, that this couldn't be happening, that it was unreal—like a film.

But this was no film, this was for real.

'Help! Help! Oh God help! Can you hear me! Please, someone send for a doctor!'

The second or third crash assured me that this was no film and also conveniently and helpfully wakened our determinedly sleeping neighbours. This was, after all, a respectable street. Things like this didn't happen to people like us; to people we knew. Well, we'd blown that one! They did and they were.

I could just make out the shape of our neighbour, a pale blur clutching a dressing gown, gazing upward in amazed bewilderment and astonishment as she made out the dark-fogged outline of my body, half hung over the window like a quilt left out to dry.

'Is anything wrong?'

Funny, how we ask the obvious in emergencies.

How to explain? I did not try.

'Please ring the doctor quickly. His name's Doctor Savage. His number's 445 1511. Tell him we need his help now. It's urgent. Please help us!'

The plump, sleep-drunk form of my neighbour's husband had joined his frightened wife amongst the suburban laurel leaves for a hurried conference. For a while there was no answer. I leaned out even more perilously. What were they saying? Would they help us? Why did they not answer?

I can guess. Perhaps they were finding it difficult to believe their eyes and ears. I was struggling with the unreality of it and I was living it, calling them to be a part of this real-life drama too. And where would it end? Perhaps they could go back to sleep, pretend it all hadn't happened, that it was a dream they'd heard, a nightmare that called in the garden. Perhaps they could return to the neat order and safety of their bedroom and the predictable pattern of their days and leave the danger, disorder and chaos that was shouting to them from the darkness of a neighbour's garden.

My ears ached as I waited for their next move.

The garage door whined on its rusty hinges. We all heard the door slam and the shot of a bolt in the back door. My strained ears heard heavy, clumsy steps, the snick of a light switch, then silence.

What was he doing, my father, in his brown, tobacco-stained dressing-gown and familiar striped pyjamas? Was he slumped in the lounge in the big, brown-covered armchair, the knife still in his hand; the tidy order, shattered by the fragments of glass from the French windows, lying round his feet. What was he thinking, alone in that broken room from which his family had fled; the wife and children barricaded in his son's bedroom; his teenage daughter half out of the window, pleading with reluctant, sleep-bemused neighbours to phone his doctor? Even now, twenty-five years later, I do not know. I expect I never will.

'Look here, now. What's the matter?' Mr Smith sounded irritated.

We were being a nuisance. We had no right to disturb a quiet neighbourhood like this. They needed their sleep. He would have to be up early in the morning for the office and look at the time, nearly three a.m. It really wouldn't do.

'Please, please, I can't explain, but ring the doctor! 445 1511. Tell him to hurry! We need help and Mum's ill as well.'

Hanging over the window-sill is not the best place for explanations but it does lend a certain urgency to one's requests.

The tired, white-worried faces withdrew into the night. Each minute dragged itself by. Each second a long-drawn-out-aching wait. The minutes loudly ticked themselves off on the clock. Five minutes. Ten. Surely help must come soon. We were too tired to speak, and what was there to say? Feet were stared at, or each other's strained faces, or the carpet. Its floral pattern began to dance in front of my eyes. My tall, lanky brother sat on a chair, his back to the big wardrobe with which he had blocked the door. My mother lay on the bed, a hand pressed to her chest, her heart racing at treble its normal speed. Years of strain had made the heart run, pounding out its message of fear till she heard little else. I sat on the dressing-table stool, watching my mother's face. She did not look at me, nor could I guess her thoughts. So we sat and waited.

Brr. Brr . . . Brr Brr.

Silence.

Brr Brr . . . Brr Brr . . .' It demanded to be answered. On and on it rang. We sat as if we had seen the Gorgon's head. Still it rang and then, abruptly, stopped.

Why hadn't the doctor come? We could not answer the phone enquiry, helpless behind the door that we had sealed, which now also cut us off from those who might break through our nightmare to cut us free. I suppose our elderly doctor had cursed the phone breaking his dreams and had wearily let the receiver rest, before dialling our number to enquire why on earth we hadn't phoned ourselves, and what on earth was going on? So many calls . . . many unnecessary . . . and he was so tired. It was cold and he wasn't as young as he once was.

The clock made a small click. Four a.m. The minutes shivered by.

'Please, Doctor Savage, please come!'

Brr Brr. Brr Brr . . .

Oh not again! How hard it was not to answer, to sit and hear it ring. In my youth and ignorance, in my fear and desperation, I sat and cursed the doctor who would not come.

Four-thirty. My toes were so cold. Then all was changed. Something had told that doctor in his cold, four-o'clock-room that he needed to get up, that this emergency call was indeed one that needed his attention. The rest of the night is a confused jumble: the crunch of car wheels on gravel, the blue flash of a police light . . . a quiet, firm, disembodied voice calling from the garden.

'Mr David . . . Mr David! Open the door!'

Policemen standing in the hall. My father still carrying the dull, long-bladed kitchen knife; his bulk suddenly shrunk within the faded, brown dressing-gown. My father suddenly grown old, grey, stubbled jaw, mumbling incoherently through slurred lips. My mother gasping for breath as we hurriedly packed a few things, and then a dazed drive, a single porch light, and a shared double bed at my mother's friend's house.

Chapter 10

Laugh and the world laughs with you;
Weep, and you weep alone . . .

So said the neatly smiling face of my mother's friend. It is both true and untrue. There have been times when I have wept bitter, desperate tears in front of a stranger and known myself understood and that I was not alone in my search to find a way beyond pain to a place where I could breathe. It was not easy. But sometimes the way out is the way through. And if someone has been that way and knows it, you know. You know when another human being is with you and for you in that search. You know. There are times when I have cried with a friend and a husband and known myself alone. There are times when I have wept alone in an empty house. I am not sure which is the most lonely. The last, though hard, is the most truthful and the pain in a way is thereby the cleaner. There are many times when I have refused to cry, when I have stopped the tide of grief and said, like King Canute, 'Stop, go back!' Fool that I was, to say to the waves, desist. They just went underground and the pressure of that forbidding did indeed whisper to my heart to bid it break. There are times when it is wise to go with the inner wind.

Three days and three nights I had walked, white-faced, cold as a corpse. I would not, could not cry. The world and its doings were on a separate track; no connection. My mother's friend, in the hardness of her quotation, did me a favour. I must have looked quite odd, pale stiff ghost that I was. I expect she'd hoped that I would snap out of it. In fact I did the opposite; I snapped into it. I always was a contrary child. It was, however, exactly what I needed. What we want and what we need, I have learnt from bitter experience, are rarely one and the same thing. We usually, eventually, get what we need. We often do not get what we want or, when we do, we discover it wasn't what we'd thought after all. We then have to go in search of what we need and have all the bother of retracing our steps. Still, I suppose it's better late than never.

Yes, I had heard right. There it was again. 'Laugh and the world laughs with you; weep and you weep alone.' I wisely decided that the face that said the words was a part of the world it spoke about, and so ran from both. There wasn't far to go but as far as I could I ran. I ran to the end of a long garden. It would have to do. At a fence I stopped. The hoarded tears shook me in a ferocity of fear and anger. They tore at the throat in their eagerness to be free, sweeping grief before them. They wailed their lament to the listening garden. I wept for the father I had lost; for the shining image of the father of children, the father at whose feet I had listened to the music that had leapt at the fire-lit walls and warmed me through the long nights on my hospital bed. I wept for the father changed now in memory to a picture stained and twisted. I wept in fear of the future that stretched before me, faceless and voiceless. I wept because I was not sorry that my father was alone.

Locked away in a hospital bed, my father was trying not to see, trying not to know that the blackness in his mind had eaten away at his family till it had disintegrated in bitter pieces at his feet. He had sown the wind. He was now reaping the whirlwind of our judgement and our flight.

In the end one comes to the end of crying.

At another house my brother, alone in company, had also wept, slumped across a table. His tears soaked the crisp, carefully-ironed tablecloth into bedraggled creases. I have never seen my brother cry.

Quiet at last I returned to the double bed and slept and slept and slept.

Plans were laid in hurried conferences. My evident unhappiness, aloofness and isolation was 'upsetting the children'. We would have to go.

My mother went to a friend in Canterbury. My brother stayed with Doris of the white hair and comfortable face, who had always had a soft spot for 'our Andy'. I went to a relative by marriage, in an elegant, spacious house in Cheshire.

Life went on. It always does. I'm glad it does, now. Most of the time I'm glad. One day I hope to be glad, always. You might want to stop the world but you can't get off, which I think is a good thing.

The world turns and turns, circling on through the blackness of space, apparently oblivious to a cry or the stopping of a cry.

O-levels loomed, came and went, somehow dealt with by academic habit. The bright summer sun of examination time was punctured by ony two incidents.

I sat in the glossy sunshine pouring through leaded windows onto fragile flowers and stalwart furniture, in my borrowed room. I saw my father's figure plodding its weary way up the graceful, tree-lined drive.

The door-bell rang. Voices exchanged a question and answer. The door was shut and my father's body retreated down the curving path.

He had left a record, neatly, carefully wrapped and tied with string. A peace-offering to try to bridge the chasm that now gaped so wide. He was sent away. His daughter did not want to see him. His flesh and blood had requested that he be excluded, shut out by a door and a word.

What did he think as he waded down the neat shrub-lined path and shut the ornamental gate, knowing that the eyes of his daughter were watching, willing him to leave? I sat on, suddenly freezing cold in the sunshine on that summer's day. My father's body disappeared from view but that retreating image lived on.

To live in a stranger's house is not easy. I was 'lucky'. At least I had a house to live in. They were kind and generous; generous of their time, of their home and food, of their own freedom. They were no longer their own family. They were no longer alone: there was a stranger within their gates. I was no longer free to retreat into grief, moodiness or irritability. To be always polite and helpful, ever ready to wash the crockery and to set the table, was a strain that is hard to imagine from such little things.

As I was coming out of an examination I was handed a letter by a member of staff. It was odd to get a personal letter in school: usually home and school were kept in exclusive compartments. It was easier that way.

It was a message from my mother. The court hearing had been postponed for another month to six weeks. Six more weeks of separation; of loneliness in a friendly stranger's house. As I stood outside a classroom in the grey-clad line of my class. I tried desperately to rearrange my face. Oh, how to stop it crumpling into the tears of a desperately disappointed child?

Our diminutive, hawk-faced headmistress passed by the line of waiting girls and saw the crumpled eyes. She had eyes to see.

Strange it is how often we see and don't see, hear and don't hear. On second thoughts it's not so strange after all. It has been so since the world began, and all the teachers of wisdom have told and warned us so. It has only taken me forty years to learn it from inside myself—that there is also a time for seeing and a time for hearing. Truth is of the light and light, when concentrated, can cut to the core. We are only flesh and blood, or rather we are also flesh and blood and frail as the flowers of the field. God is merciful. There is a waiting and a watching. When we are ready, the Word goes out, the veil is drawn aside . . . Then we have a chance to see, to see clearer, and with that comes a choice. Then it's up to us.

An authoritative wave of the hand and I was drawn from the waiting line and ushered quietly to her office.

'What's the matter?' The deep-set eyes were clear, unblinking. I answered to the close-cut, self-effacing olive carpet at my feet. 'We've got to wait longer for the court-hearing . . . and . . . and I want to go home . . . but there's no home to go to . . . I want our own front door . . . and Mum's miles away. I haven't seen her for *ages.* It's weeks now.' The adult facade disappeared into water at my feet, staining the official carpet with human grief.

When the tears had been absorbed by the sun-filled quiet air, the little-hawk-headmistress had explained that you see . . . she had so wanted to offer me shelter . . . but . . . you see, she could not, it would create talk, of unprofessionalism, of favouritism, of inappropriate behaviour . . . It was so difficult, she wished it had been possible. My art mistress had wanted to do the same. They did feel for me . . . she was sure I would understand. I did.

A drop of understanding goes a long way in a desert.

Two months later we had a home again; not quite our own place but a house, four walls and a roof, rooms in which to sleep and sing, to work and rest, to eat and play: a front door to shut on the world.

This time the inner world was a safe one, predictable and calm. No longer did my stomach lurch as I put the key in the door, wondering what mood my father was in this time. No longer would my stomach flinch at words with razor edges.

Celebrations and festivals had once been mined with anger, frustration, hate. Now we could enjoy birthdays and secular Christmas in peace. We might even invite someone in, as now we had no avenging ghost to frighten the guests away long before the witching hour of the night.

My birthday presumably coincidentally had always brought on a fit of anger in my father. Nowadays I do not believe in luck or coincidence. The coinciding of two events in time is an interesting juxtaposition that is well worth our attention. Especially if they regularly occur. My scientific mind had not been trained to take in such patterning of events or to seek their meaning. So much the better for me. I was not ready for it. When I was ready the meaning came.

Year by year I longed for a party of my own, something to which I could invite some acquaintances from school. Other girls had parties. I thirsted and hungered to be the same. I was a long time learning. One year we tried it; once and once only.

The dutiful flock of gaily-clad-party-frock-wrapped children came through the door. An hour later we were all congregated in the garden, assembled by brother and mother for the ritual party games. Things were almost normal.

My father wasn't there, of course, because he was upstairs, sleeping as usual. Still, fathers couldn't always be at their daughters' birthday parties, could they? Some were away on business sometimes and no one knew about my Dad . . . yet. So far I was safe, his absence unremarked.

A door slammed, thrown against its hinges by an angry, sullen wind. My father's round and crumpled form, encased in its bedraggled, dirty, washed-out, brown dressing-gown, lumbered through the French windows, which slammed to in his wake. Hot words were hurled at my mother's embarrassed face. My brother stood stiffly at her side, his eyes on the grass at his feet, the party-games book hanging limply from his hand. Silence swirled and eddied round the suburban garden. The door banged again. My father was gone. The party was over.

I never had a party again.

One year I had been thrilled to receive quite a number of Christmas cards from my classmates. Always a loner, I was especially delighted to have a small mound of richly coloured cards to bring home as trophies of my acceptance at last by the group. Carefully I arranged them side by side on the mantlepiece of the breakfast room. Every time I went in the room I looked at them. They were better than any present. Christmas had come, perhaps goodwill did abound after all.

When I came downstairs on Christmas Eve I found my cards, my precious cards, in bits: torn to shreds and scattered round the room.

I left them there and didn't tidy them away. When my father came downstairs—eventually—he avoided the question of my face and the bits of coloured paper lying mute on the floor. He sat hunched, crunching the Kellogg's cornflakes. The only sound for a while was of teeth on cereal.

'Dad, what's happened to the cards . . . *my* cards?'

Why did I ask? I knew. I knew.

'Oh shut up . . . Why should you be the one to enjoy yourself!'

Tears gave me courage.

'You'd no right. No right! They were mine, mine! Given to *me* to wish me Happy Christmas!'

Brave no longer, I fled the room leaving him to the silence and the crunch of Kellogg's, the gaily-coloured pieces around his feet.

What is it about Christmas, about Christ's mass, about the celebration of the birth of a baby—a baby who was both the same but different? That baby has changed history, made history, and altered my own. Why is this day different from all other days? My heart asked the same question but without the words. The answer to the one is I think the answer to the other. The connection has taken me twenty years to discover.

Now I hoped and longed for a special Christmas, for beribboned boxes and parcels; for jokes and singing. Year after year I hoarded my coins and planned for presents that would brighten the eyes. Year by year I would come down the stairs on Christmas morning, my pillow-case bulging with parcels and packets. Softly opening the door I would solemnly and ceremoniously place each person's particular present by their plate. My mother's face would be tight, shuttered with anxiety. My brother frowned down his long nose, pleased, embarrassed.

My father would unwrap his present with slow, unexcited hands.

'Very nice . . .' The voice was dead, the much-thought-over parcel put aside. The mouth ate on. 'What the hell, I'm no good, no damn good.'

The door thuds to a close.

Silence.

Another Christmas was put away in its battered cardboard box, the tinsel tarnished and broken, but the dream lived on.

'I'm dreaming of a white Christmas . . .' The image of snow-encrusted houses, sparkling in the clear, cold air, was not all of it, that much I knew. There was something about Christmas that haunted me. I longed for the spirit of Christmas to come to drive out the misery of the house. There was no Jewish Festival that was like it. Its magic was unique. As the years of my body grew, so did the longing. I listened for a sound I could not hear. One day I was to hear it. The dream was to come true, but in a way I did not expect.

Another Christmas came. I was too old to play Father Christmas with his bulging-pillow-case sack. Instead I went for long star-lit walks. The suburban streets smelt different at night; as if the earth were waking. The quiet was friendly. The sight of lighted Christmas trees in the darkened windows along the road drew me then and holds me still . . . Light in the dark . . . coloured lights held against the night.

Mesmerised by their magic, I had pestered my mother to buy a little tree to plant in our heirloom-purple-pot in the breakfast room. Perhaps the magic circle could be in our house too.

The tree did its best; its arms stiffly erect, holding our new tinsel and lovingly, hopefully-bought baubles, but the magic circle that I wanted did not light the room. The symbol and the reality it points to must come together for that, but at least it was there: a little tree, a little, brave, hopeful signpost to a way beyond the dark. I have needed that little tree since. It has lit the dark for me when the light was going out on another Christmas Eve. I have the tree still. It was only tiny then, now it has grown big and strong, its branches green with new growth. When it was as small as my son, I sat in the dark and watched the fairy lights glimmer in the shadows. I rocked and rocked my whimpering son to the light of that stalwart, hopeful tree. It kept me alive. I have reason to be grateful to that tree and the centuries of hope that grew it as a symbol to be set against the death of winter. I have a great respect for symbols nowadays.

Then, in the safety of another house, in the kitchen, helping my mother in her last minute preparations for the traditional, secular Midwinter feast, I heard the sound of singing down the road. Without a word of explanation, with flour-covered hands and aproned waist, I went out of the gate to hear the carol singers move from lamp to lamp as they sang to the waiting air and the people in their busy, shuttered houses. I was the only one who stood at the gate and listened. The music, packed with centuries of faith and awe and wonder, passed the closed-off path. The gloved and muffled people who gave it voice moved slowly by with a nod and a smile. Like the children of Hamelin, I longed to follow the Pied Piper down snow-filled paths, but my feet were still on the tarmac path. This was no fairy story. I leaned on the gate, my throat tight, my eyes hot. I did not know why I wept. Angry with myself, I dashed the tears aside, straightened my mouth and went inside.

Chapter 11

a call echoed down the corridors of time,
lying at my feet it coiled in sleep,
till at a summons it awoke.
At the blaze of your voice
I warmed my hands, took off my shoes and knelt.

Ordinary level examinations had been passed and the world was now pieced together in a new pattern. No longer did the heart lurch as the latch was lifted on going home. At school I was now freed to study in depth the subjects that I loved, English, History and Art. Interesting how threes are there even in the academic life. The three are closely connected: all interested in the patterning of life and of interrelationships. Not that my teachers saw it quite like that.

We were only the second year of a selective intake in the new Technical school. Our year was the first to attempt a number of Advanced level examinations. Fifteen students were attempting the three advanced exams necessary for university applications. The teachers were released, like us. Daring to be people, we sat together, questioning, disputing, on a voyage of mutual discovery. I wonder if we had all had more courage, whether all the years of education could have had that atmosphere. To emerge from behind the role, from behind the word 'Teacher', to become just a You, a Self, learning with other selves, sharing the glimpses of truth and meaning found so far, that would take courage indeed, more than it sounds. I know . . . I've tried it. Barriers make for safety as well as defence. Take them down and the waves may roll in too high. We may get out of our depth, so the sea wall is kept in place. In the schools now the sea wall's crumbling under the onslaught of the tidal wave. The bluff's been called and the wall is almost down in places. But the sea is angry now and I tremble for the men and women who are trying to hold the weight of water back.

The History mistress would enter the class and firmly and decisively place the textbook on the desk. 'Sue, no questions today. We really *must get on with the syllabus!*'

Hour by sun-saturated hour was spent drawing and designing in the Art rooms with only two of us to one member of staff. It was like being apprenticed to master craftsmen. We were taught how to transfer designs from the mind to paper, first to plastic then onto a screen which, when printed, reproduced our original, mental images onto cloth, according to our accuracy, skill and patience.

The satisfaction and fulfilment of making something with my hands and mind, a tangible thing that exists as an objective reality in the outer world, began here; it has never left me. To say, 'It is good; this is a child of my brain and hand; I made it; it would not exist apart from my thought and skill', is indeed in some microcosm to be like God . . .

So this created being thought and slept, read, worked, drew and painted. In studying the structure of flowers and plants I struggled to train the hand to catch their intricate mystery and interrelated harmony in line and colour. I studied the 'Old Masters' and through the created universe and through human creation, I was forced again and again to ask the old, old questions.

In a sense such questions always continue. They do not end till we end and perhaps not even then. As we struggle to answer them we just dig deeper, wider; go further in and further on.

I knew that no work of art just 'happens' . . . no interplay of blind forces here. Could the rich splendours of the earth, pulsating with rhythm and many-coloured life, be the product of a mindless juxtaposition of molecules? Like the eighteenth-century philosophers before me, I asked what was the first cause? In the beginning, what was there? And did these questions have any relevance or reality to this speck of dust breathing in the immensity of space?

The drawings and paintings of Leonardo would draw me to them, a secret addiction to which I returned again and again and again. In Leonardo da Vinci's work I saw a child who was young yet old in his eyes, and women who knew the secret of the stars, who stared at the living and beyond the dead. Here were women who held their secret close, like . . . like the child in their lap.

This man, multi-faceted: painter, scientist and courtier, the Renaissance man, reaching to the skies, was not at peace. He was restless, discontented, confined and imprisoned within the different media of his work. Nothing could quite satisfy the hungry enquiry of his search to extend the boundaries of paint. In this one life was some of the very nature of all men.

'The Madonna of the Rocks' was the last painting I looked at, always. Head propped on uniformed arms, I stared and stared at the faces of the woman and the angel that pointed to the young-old child. If only I could unblock the barrier that was in my ears, I would hear the word that hovered on the edge of hearing. My ears strained to catch the word; my mind and eyes ached with the effort to catch it, but the answer did not come and, with a sigh, the book would be slowly shut; the mystery covered once more and the book silent like the skies.

Holidays came. My mother and I would ferret out the

local churches, the older the better. Sketch pad in hand I would catch the pattern of window and wood-carving, snaring the thoughts of bygone artists onto obedient paper. For a while I would be engrossed in detail, forgetting the whole in the interest of the past. Then the heavy, waiting quiet would catch my breath and still the hand, demanding attention.

Together, mother and daughter stood in the nave of a silent church, listening, waiting . . . for what? We did not know.

Trespassing on forbidden territory I tiptoed on careful feet, over time-rounded polished stone, to stare at a half-naked man, nailed to his pieces of wood, pinned against the sky. His face was always sad, stretched tight with pain, but never anger-flecked, bitter or defiant. Why didn't that mouth shout oaths and curses to the crimson air? I remembered Mercutio's despairing shout at the laughter-sick and howling mob . . .

'A plague on both your houses!'

Why had this bent and twisted shape become the Christian symbol? The image was now in my dreams awake or asleep.

Turning my back on the crippled, dying man, I listened again. The air was full and heavy with the knowledge of the angel and the woman and the twisted man. The emptiness was thick with it.

Taking the arm of my patient mother, we would be released into the painful-bright sunlight. The synagogue was not like this, did not feel like this.

'They are beautiful . . . churches . . .'

What did she think, my mother? Did she sense in her bones that I was to become the forbidden thing—the outcast—the goat in the desert?

One Saturday, many months before, I had waited behind to see if the synagogue, empty of its people, with only the lamp, the everlasting light of the covenant which burned day and night over the ark alight in the gloom, would have some sense of hidden knowledge, as did those other places of worship. It was that sense of the Other tht drew me like a moth to the candle. I could not keep away. Would that sense of the Other be here for me? The well-dressed, chattering crowd could only now be heard behind the polished doors, but the silence left did not feel the same. It was a silence that was the absence of noise, nothing more. It had a different quality, a different feel. This was a quiet, empty building; four walls and a roof. The shiny door swung to and fro behind me.

I was a Jew: a Jew whose tradition now taught that to fulfil the laws and customs of the race was to fulfil the obligations bound upon you by your Jewish birth; that this in itself was what was required by and pleasing to God. But I was not content to believe because I was told. I wanted to find out for myself. I still do. A leopard does not change its spots.

If it is findable out, I want to know: to discover for myself—to be able to say I know of my experience that this is so—to know because I know. It has got me into a lot of trouble over the years. Perhaps such cussedness always will. But perhaps also there is good in it and some strength. Explorers may need to be cussed. And at the end we may all be a little wiser; the boundaries of knowledge having been extended. For it seems to me that if there is knowledge to be had in this area of life, knowledge that is, not belief, then it is the only knowledge worth having: a knowledge that lives and works and can be known. Books are usually only guides and maps; the recordings of a journey that has been made. It can make interesting reading to read about another country in a book but it's nothing like actually going there for yourself.

But how could I be sure such a God existed to be pleased

or placated by obedience to the old traditions? How could finite humanity, with its mortal, time-bound mind grasp the nature or existence of the immortal; the infinite, who existed beyond the dimensions of time and space? My brain ached with the attempt even to grasp the implications of the question, never mind any of the answers! No, I was not content. An inner restlessness, an imperative within drove me on. It still does; an uncomfortable companion.

In search of truth and proof of claims regarding this precious commodity called faith, that I realised I was singularly without, I decided to see the rabbi.

His black-robed figure had intoned and chanted, unchanged by the noiseless passing of the years. His hands had been raised in blessing over the bent head of my brother at his *Barmitzvah*, when he had come of age and accepted for himself the rights and obligations of his Jewish heritage. Stiff with pride and jealousy I had watched the rabbi's hands guide with silver pointer my brother's careful eyes from Hebrew word to Hebrew word, as his boy's voice took the place of the honoured man appointed to read a portion of the Law from the sacred, heavy scroll.

I was given no chance, as a girl, ceremoniously to take upon myself the pains and duties, the distinctions and separation, of Jewish womanhood. For me there had been no instruction in the Law and the writings of my people. In the reading and the studying of the Law there was no place for women. Well I would seek out the teacher for myself, the rabbi, and see what he could give me of the wisdom of the ages. What would he teach me concerning the faith of my forebears and how one could find the living core upon which the traditions were built? Most of all I wanted to know the reasons for his belief; the causes of his faith and their effects in day-to-day existence. With nothing else in my hand I arrived, alone, at the synagogue. This time not on the Sabbath.

Pausing a moment for breath and courage, I knocked at the neatly-labelled highly-polished office door.

'Come in.' The voice was even-toned, official.

'Good morning. What can I do for you?' It sounded like the doctor, except there was no visible prescription pad.

I sat uneasily on the edge of the squeakily protesting, plump leather armchair. I looked at the heavy desk and blinded window and the city-suited man with the silver pencil in thick fingers.

How to begin? How did one start such things? What was I starting? Being a 'splosh-into-the-deep-end' sort, I thought I may as well plunge in.

'Is there a God . . . is there a God . . . do you believe there is a God . . . who . . . speaks . . .?

The question felt like a blundering intrusion into the neat, city office, with its bland, official face. I was embarrassed by the way the sound of it fell into the space between . . .

I wanted to ask, 'Is there anything anywhere . . . is there point in life worth the struggle, the pain. Does what we do matter . . .?' I asked nothing, nothing but the first, because in the first question lay all the others. The others we ask in one form or another of the doctor now, not the priest . . .

The silence spread to my feet. I examined the scuffed polish of my shoes with desperate interest. A fly buzzed as desperately against the blind that blocked its exit to freedom.

'You have to have faith to believe.'

I raised my eyes and examined the thick, wide fingers, balancing now against each other; the pen left in its carved, stone cocoon. I longed to take my anger out and splash it across the discreetly coloured walls and the stiff air.

I am here because I have no faith. How can you command such a thing! I need answers. I need answers that will stand strong in the cold winds that blow, inside and out . . . and you command me to have faith, plucked magically from a hidden tree and swallowed without a thought!

I said nothing.

My sullen, angry, hungry face must have demanded more than I had the courage to ask. Words were quietly, carefully, piled upon words. I should join the choir, observe the rituals. I had a chip on my shoulder because of what had happened in my family. I should observe the customs, the Sabbaths . . . faith would come . . .

No words touched the centre; they fell, weak and lifeless onto the expensive, green-piled carpet.

That was all. Silent and furious, I rose to leave; the tangle of questions still folded and packed in my head . . . 'The situation, the difficulties, the upsets . . .' What did he know? If only he knew, if only he could feel it; the nightmare at your heels, wailing . . .

The door shut with a gentle click. A different door had been closed than the one of polished wood.

Chapter 12

There are times when, to my shame, I have been ashamed of being a teacher. When people asked me in the street, or on meeting an acquaintance of my mother's I was asked, 'Oh what do you do?' and I said, 'I'm a teacher,' their eyes would cloud over and slide away with a shrug and a polite smile. Without knowledge or enquiry, I am appraised, weighed in the balance and found wanting. 'Those who can, do, and those who can't, teach.' I am dismissed along with the work, my experience, and all that I have learnt.

When I think of the teacher and the taught, again and again some lines of Robert Bolt's play *A Man for all Seasons* keep turning and turning in my mind. I think of them still, when I wonder whether all was well done and whether some day I will return to the barricades. The words sound in the mind like a gong, the shiver and shake of its note spreading wider and wider . . . out and out and out . . .

Says Thomas More to Richard Rich, a poor scholar, who longs for preferment, for power and status and influence and to move amongst the rich and famous:

> 'But, Richard, in office they offer you all sorts of things. I was once offered a whole village, with a mill and a manor house, and heaven knows what else—a coat of arms I shouldn't be surprised. Why not be a teacher? You'd be a fine teacher. Perhaps a great one.'
>
> 'And if I was who would know it?'

'You, your pupils, your friends, God. Not a bad public, that.'

I have been a teacher. I have loved it and hated it. I have had joy and suffering. I have learnt an immense amount from it. There are those who teach who are not teachers. There are teachers who teach words from a page. There are those who have knowledge and not wisdom. There are those who love knowledge but not children. Why do we respect knowledge, when it is on a page, in a chart or diagram, but do not see that that insight, that knowledge and understanding of a secret within the universe, was discovered by the minds of those who as children came before the men and women who gave that understanding its birth.

'Those who can, do, and those who can't, teach.' There's a truth in that quotation as in all sayings old and new, otherwise they wouldn't have been made, but it is, I believe, only a half truth. It is a half truth that bedevilled my own quest for a pattern of life that was in keeping with what was within me at that time.

Now my concept of the teacher and the taught has broken out of its bounds. Perhaps I am a teacher still; without doubt I am a student. The teachers and the taught come in many guises and are experienced in many modes. To teach you have to know, to understand; perhaps even to love. To learn, you have to believe, you have to be open to change, you have to desire wisdom and insight and knowledge. To be a teacher you have to have desired and to desire wisdom and insight and knowledge. You have to be open to change; you have to be able to listen and believe that what you are doing is worth the doing. The teacher and the taught: are they so different?

What is it truly to teach? Can you teach falsely? I think so. How is the one distinguished from the other? By a quality and a good hard look at the vision and the facts that are given to us. Between the vision and the facts are the gaps. It is as well to be aware of them. If you are not on the look-out you can fall through gaps. Whether or not there will be something to land on if you fall through the black hole of the gap is a matter of conjecture. It may not always be wise to experiment. You never know what you may land on. The new terrain may be nothing like the old. Falling down holes may be quite an uncomfortable if not an outright dangerous experience. Needless to say I have fallen down the odd hole myself, complete with appropriate sets of bruises to remind me I've been there. The exploration of space can be an internal as well as an external fact. The deeper in you go the bigger it gets.

The role of seer and prophet and teacher are far more inextricably linked than at first may be apparent. It is said that the people perish when there is no vision. But even a vision may not be enough. It is witnesses now that we need. It is not sufficient to be prophet and seer; the vision must be lived first. The vision will need to stand up to the test of fire and water and pain. It is the living that comes before the showing and the telling. You have to have something to say before you search for the words to tell it in, to tell it true.

Always, but always, there is the great gulf fixed, between the knowing about and the knowing that is of itself: that is of the real. It is the second knowing that can sometimes knock us between the eyes with its quiet, irrefutable touch. We know when we know, although it may take us years then to catch up with that knowing and understand it.

A teacher changed my life and in the fullness of time I became a teacher. In the fullness of time students told me I had changed their lives. They were not the same as they had been; the world and their perception of it had shifted to a different balance. So I was told. It's a dangerous occupation, teaching, sometimes literally. Real teaching is dangerous. It all depends how close to the wind you sail. It rocks the boat—your own and others. Socrates was killed for it. It has been known to happen to others. Truth changes the teachers and the taught. It is 'not a tame lion'!

'It is a fearful thing to fall into the hands of the living God.'

You can say that again!

So for me, how did this 'falling' come about? It began by the 'falling through' of some long-held views on the boring nature of RE lessons. I'd given up on them and wangled my way to extra Art instead. It seemed that they had not, however, given up on me.

My classmates waxed long and eloquent on the amazing interest of RE lessons with this new teacher. For my classmates to wax long and eloquent and totally spontaneously about any lesson whatsoever under the sun was miracle in itself. Something was up; something had changed. It had indeed! What I didn't know was that I was next on the hit list.

By what was I going to be hit? By the power of knowing; of experiencing and hearing that inner knowledge at work within the mode of the story. It was at the door. You have to be careful if you get too near a living story. You can't be too sure what it might do next. If you don't watch out it just might ask you a question. Still, if it does you can always try the traditional rabbinical method of answering a question with a question. It's useful as a delay or even as an evasion whilst you catch your breath. The trouble is that of course one thing leads to another and before you know you're somewhere other than where you started out, and questions and answers come to your mind that you can never unhear. The trouble with questions is that they have the unfortunate habit of pulling you towards answers . . . or at least the beginnings of them. The trouble with the answers, even the beginnings of ones, is that they frequently are not what you expect. Suddenly you have moved from one world to the next. The jet-lag between the two can be quite unnerving, if not just plain exhausting. There is such a thing as getting more than you bargained for!

An RE lesson that was interesting would have to be experienced to be believed—a useful adage that, but a dangerous one. Give that sort of challenge to Life and invariably, in my experience, before long you are answered. Experience can be quite unsettling.

I was, unknowingly, about to be thoroughly unsettled.

So I went to listen to some stories. What I didn't know was that I was going to listen to the real thing. There should have been a sign on the door saying, 'Danger, Keep Out!' Instead my classmates said quite truthfully, 'It's really interesting, come in!' So I did—in more ways than one.

I had used a precious free period to join the lesson, to find out if it was fact or fiction, this difference, this lesson that was like no other. Just for once I said to myself, just this once. 'I'll try anything once . . .' Old Testament of course. Also of course, I joined the back row—a sign of noncommitment and potential challenge; my chair finely balanced against the wall; my arms folded against my chest. I can't remember all that was said but I remember the gist and its impact on me, even thirty years later. My class was right.

Who was the vehicle of this astonishing fact of a lesson on religion that was interesting? Who was this teacher, this seer? . . . A little woman; a tiny woman, with small pointed face and heavy eyes, that looked at you as if out of a medieval painting. The body was scaled down to size, dainty, a little thick around the waist, Crimplene suit and grey-brown-crinkle-chipped hair in corrugated folds around the high forehead, but the voice was deep, quiet: a commanding voice. The voice was the voice of a forest pool, still, quiet, dangerous.

The lesson was on Gideon. It was the implications that

were so astonishing, worrying and totally unsettling for a thorough twentieth-century rationalist like myself. I'm still struggling with the consequences of the questions I began to ask and the beginnings of the answers I began to hear in that lesson.

Jew that I was, I remembered nothing of Gideon or his doings, or why he should have been immortalised, his life being recorded in this book of books. This book was only useful to me for its physical width, depth and weight. I had used it to press flowers with; to prop up other books with when doing homework. I had used it to act as a door-stop or table-balancer; or more usually as a book-end and collector of dust.

I had tried to read it once, but had given up after the first chapter. Even the first verse was bad enough: 'In the beginning God . . .' There it was, Mount Everest, unclimbable, almost—just there; plonked without so much as a by-your-leave, no explanation, no background as to why it should be there; this great, jagged mountain slap-bang in the way across the middle of the world. What a statement! What a claim! If it was so, the whole world shifted into a different balance. If it wasn't, all is meaningless; nothing matters and there is no good or bad, only thinking makes it so. 'In the beginning God . . .' and on this all else is balanced; all rests. It is a statement and a claim that is the fulcrum point of the Universe: the pivot point of all pain and prayer and searching for truth. One way or another it is behind and beneath and within all things.

I could not make that quantum leap of thought. Perhaps the Mount Everest was just a mirage, an illusion in a dry and thirsty land where no water was. The few people I knew who made such a leap assumed the existence of God as the beginning and basis on which their religion was built. When cross-examined the usual response was something like, 'Well, there just has to be something . . .'. I did not see that there had to be anything, anything at all.

No one I knew read this book seriously for profit or pleasure, unless they had to for an examination, yet here was a woman, a musician, who seemed to know everything there was to know about Gideon and more.

My chair bumped into a perpendicular position with a thump and a protesting groan. This ancient character was a living, breathing, struggling, uncertain human being. He was being called, spoken to, and there was no one there. He, Gideon, himself was being called, himself and not another. This was not how he had been taught, this was not what he expected; this was not how he had been reared. He was the least; he was the youngest and it was to him that the voice spoke. Life wasn't like that, but suddenly it was. He asked for a sign and the sign was given. He tried to make it difficult for the voice but the difficulty removed itself. The world tilted and shifted out of balance. It moved alarmingly into a new configuration. It was all most unsettling. I know the feeling.

The words of the story had power, because young as I was I knew that this story was no story only; that this story was told in such a way by a human being who knew of what it spoke. I had had my first living proof of the two different forms of knowing. This woman knew something from the inside. I knew without being told that this woman had heard this voice speak. This medieval-twentieth-century-face had heard the outside-inside voice that could speak in the dark.

Many months and hours filled with questions and dispute lay ahead and then my own time came.

One day it was said; the figure lurking in my mind; the man I saw nailed against the sky-beyond the image—the voice spoke. As ever, it was not when I expected it; I was off guard for a moment. I thought I was safe, tucked in a corner, listening to someone else's question for a change.

But the time was up. The challenge this time was thrown at my feet . . . I did not want to hear.

After the earthquake, the wind and the fire . . . the still small voice . . .

In a coffee bar, a fellow student asked how many chances do we have to hear, to find our way and to be found? There was time, lots of time, time enough to think of these things. She would go to college, have fun, maybe think on these imponderables later, when she was older, but not now, then . . . maybe . . .

And in the pause for breath it came. Still, quiet, inaudible but loud—I could not but hear it.

'It is now for you. For you the time is now.'

I had sown the wind; I was beginning to reap the whirlwind. I had asked and now I was answered and asked of. It was most inconvenient. Are the things of God ever convenient? I doubt it. I had been asked. What would I answer? What would I do? I foresaw trouble ahead. In that I was profoundly right.

Chapter 13

So what was it like to cross the Equator: to move from one hemisphere to another? It was so simple, so deceptively simple; dangerously simple. It was so simple that at first I did not believe it, so great is the twentieth century respect for complexity and the demonstrable, scientifically, laboratory provable.

A girl knelt by a bed. Silent words were spoken in the inner air. I made a request. The call and the question was returned to its unseen source. If God was . . . I wanted to know; to hear; to learn. If this . . . this . . . Christ whom I had read about was indeed a living force within time and eternity, a fulcrum point within the seen and unseen universe, then I wanted to become a part of his Way. To the centre of life that is at the core of all, an invitation and a call was made by one small speck of living dust that walked on two legs on this circling planet, wheeling through the dark of space. I waited to see what would happen. I did not have to wait long.

I had thought that probably nothing much would change. All that had happened was that words had been spoken to the empty air. No matter that something had happened in history all those centuries ago that had convinced people that a man—an apparently unique man—had experienced a power in death to work backwards. I had thought that if this was so, then nothing was as I had previously thought.

All night I argued with myself. The silence went on.

There was no Damascus flash. But in that arguing and struggle I had crystallised a problem. Nice Jewish girls do not become Christian, becoming a traitor to their people. My family was already divided, my mother's mother very ill. In the way of God, what was right? Could I be shown whether to speak or not to speak? I did not sleep much that night.

Breakfast time arrived eventually, as it usually did at about 7.30 a.m. The cornflakes gazed at me and I at them. I pushed them reluctantly round the bowl trying to remember what books to pack for the first lesson. The question of the night before was nearly forgotten until another question nearly knocked me off the kitchen stool. Shock suspended the spoon idiotically in the air: a milk-dripping exclamation mark.

I had asked to be shown whether to speak or not. I did not expect so prompt a response.

My mother gave me a sideways, careful look.

'Sue . . . you have been thinking a lot about religion lately . . . have you . . . er . . . have you come to any conclusions then?'

There it was. I had asked; I was answered.

To my knowledge this was the only time when any metaphysical question was asked at such a time of day. Such a small thing, such a small coinciding of a prayer and a question but unusual in their juxtaposition and timing. I began, in that moment, to suspect that from now on nothing was likely to be quite the same again. In that I was right. From now on anything could happen and it quite often did.

The answer to my prayer had come rather sooner than I had anticipated.

Spoon still in mid-air, the truth was spoken, baldly; the worst first.

'I . . . I . . . think it's true . . . what the New Testament says . . . I . . . I've become a Christian.'

Carefully the spoon was put back into the now sodden cornflakes. The pattern of the cornflake mounds of brown in their rivers of milk was studied for a few painful minutes. When I looked up, my mother wept, hunched over hardening toast glazed with marmalade. Head in hands she wept for the Jewish daughter she had lost.

What could be said? 'Do not cry!' My mother had every reason to cry. I had made the wound. I could not heal it. Not then.

Not the best of beginnings.

* * *

How can you describe twenty odd years of a fumbling, wavering stagger after God. 'Odd,' is about the right word. Odd and stretching. There have been many times when I have been in need of little Roo's strengthening medicine.

What a strange experiment is prayer . . . It's an experiment that gives much food for thought. Perhaps it's all coincidence, but as a bishop was known to remark, it's noticeable that when you stop praying the coincidences stop happening. In fact just to look at the word 'coincidence' is illuminating. *Coincidence*: to coincide, to correspond in area, position or outline . . . 'Oh it's just coincidence', we say . . . but suppose the coincidences keep happening, even perhaps apparently have a regular and perceivable pattern, and that prayer seems to be instigating stimulus?

The prayer experiment gives us food for thought. Sometimes it affects my stomach as well as my head, as yet again a known and familiar pattern has dissolved to realign itself into a new shape.

'It's a crutch . . .' they say, 'religion'. I wonder what leg is supposed to be missing and what exactly is the nature of the body that is supposedly propped up. I myself find that the spirit of the living God is more likely to knock props away so that we can walk, foot by foot, step by step, to a different drumbeat. Eventually we must needs learn to walk in two dimensions at once. No easy feat, as I'm sure that Einstein would agree. The real thing is no crutch. It is a call to find a Way—to discover and then unite two worlds within the self. It is a call to live across the divisions of outside and inside: to have one foot in the temporal world and one in the eternal. No easy balancing act that. I periodically fall over into one or the other, not always knowing which is which. There is a great need for maps—up-to-date, living maps of explorers who have gone ahead to tell us of the way: to tell us what to expect, so that we can be prepared. We need explorers who will tell it true. They are in short supply.

What is the air of the new country like? Are the horizon lines so different?

Words are the go-betweens of truth. They are vibrant with life. They filter and categorise experience, crystallising, expanding, limiting and suggesting. Words . . . signs pointing beyond themselves, squiggles on a page. Nothing is certain beyond all doubt: all things can be disbelieved. All truth is mediated through human personality. Reality is filtered through the senses and given meaning and order through the mind and the heart. To know this is not to deny the possibility of an outer reality, external to the self, which operates upon it, within it as well as being affected by it.

I will tell you of some of the coincidings that have followed the way of prayer, contemplation and inner silence: a silence in which I have tried to listen to that 'still small voice' that has the disconcerting habit of turning my world upside down. The coincidings in time and meaning have become landmarks for me, monuments; signposts that tell of the route to the Celestial City. It is to these that I return in my mind, when the sky darkens and the wind blows.

But as is the nature of signposts there are long, long empty stretches of road in between; so long sometimes that you are convinced that you have lost your way, until another sign looms out of the gathering fog, and with a great sigh of relief you are on the way again.

Landmarks.

Landmarks, not surprisingly tend to appear at crisis points, turnings and crossroads. If they appear looming out of the fog at precisely these points we should not be surprised. It is their nature and their function to appear at just such divisions of the way: pointers on the road to guide us as we travel on.

The timing and juxtaposition of events can be a very interesting phenomenon. The coming together of events that seem to the participants to be meaningful, helpful even, can be dismissed if they occur only once or twice. But suppose, as the bishop said, that on the way of prayer, those meeting points come again and again and again . . .

I had prayed and I was answered. Within a week a different coming together of circumstances brought me close for the first time, knowingly, to the reality and life that I had prayed to. Again I was answered; there was indeed a response to that first so crucial prayer but it was not in the form or in the manner that I had expected or desired. That's so often the way of things on the mystic path—so I have discovered.

Seven days passed: days full of hours. On the seventh day I woke suddenly from sleep. I never wake suddenly and clearly from the sleeping state. More usually I have to haul myself towards the waking shore, with effort, determination and some difficulty. Not this day. One minute it was sleep, the next I was awake. It was early.

Brr Brr. Brr Brr.

The shrill, staccato insistent rattle of the telephone demanded attention. This was no time for listening in the dark. On went the light. And in the light the waiting.

The heavy, saddened feet of my mother went to hear the message of the journey just completed. She knew. I knew the message that awaited to be spoken through wires and plastic, through the transporting of a human voice.

'Yes . . . yes . . . I'll come as soon as I can. Thank you for all you have done . . . yes . . . yes . . . thank you . . . yes . . . I will see you later . . .'

The light from under the door enticed, spoke, although no word was said.

My mother's feet turned aside from the waiting emptiness of her room. The door opened and then was shut. A woman who was my mother sat on the edge of the bed. The daughter and the mother. The mother who was a daughter to a mother. The mother who had lost a mother.

Silence.

Then slowly, 'Why are you awake? It's very early.'

'I don't know. I just woke, then heard the telephone. Is it Granny?'

Silence.

I knew. We both knew. Nothing was said. It didn't need to be said. It was known.

'Do you believe in life after death?' My mother's face was so crumpled and creased, the lips turned tight inward over the biting teeth: teeth that shut out tears.

'Yes.'

'But why . . . how can you?'

'Because Christ rose . . .'

Silently, without a word, my mother slowly, heavily, rose to her feet and left the room. The door closed behind her without a backward glance.

It was not what she wanted but it was perhaps what she needed. What we all need if it's true: that nothing is wasted, that a unique life is not obliterated, gone into the fire or the earth and totally lost. The tale tells of one who has gone before, the first born of the dead: a human life that was and is a witness to the Way; the spirit greater than the flesh, and the flesh reordered to manifest the spirit in a form that living people could see. The body could be listened to, eaten with; it was a body that could break bread and broil fish. But all was changed and nothing was as it was. He was known and not known. He came but did not need to open doors when he came. He was the same but different, different but the same.

Life on the way of God is very much like that: different but the same, the same but different.

Death is a great teacher. We fear it perhaps, because it teaches us so much. What we forget is its inextricable link with life. It is a horror and an anathema but perhaps also a gateway and a door. It asks us questions. And the question to ask and that is asked is not 'why?' but 'what?' What will be our response? In the face of this inescapable fact to which we all move at differing rates, what will be our response? To this, one of the great challenges of life, what will we say? Not only what will be our reaction to the gauntlet laid at our feet, but also what is it: what is this dying, this death?

I have come near to it, to the outskirts of death, three times. At the perimeter-fence I have seen and known a little of the 'what' . . . I have of late given up on asking the 'why'.

Experience can be an uncomfortable teacher. The trouble with experience is that it cannot be quantified, examined by microscope, scalpel or camera. In the recent visions of the Virgin Mary, reported in the *Sunday Times* on 6 October 1985, a group of five youngsters in the village of Medjugorje in Yugoslavia experienced many visions of the Virgin before many witnesses. The four who still see her at the same time each night, 6.45 p.m., have been wired up to all the scientific, diagnostic and investigative machinery available to western technology. All that can be shown is that the four are in some altered state physically, whilst the experience of the vision lasts. The experience that they say they all see simultaneously is, indeed, something that does simultaneously alter the state of their bodies in a way that can be known scientifically and measured by instruments. But what that experience is in its content and meaning can only be known by the subjective experience of the inner consciousness in the minds and hearts of the young people concerned.

To decide whether such reports are accurate and true will depend on the use of both scientific and other criteria. For example, in normal circumstances, is their account and those of their witnesses such that they would be regarded as reliable, honest and trustworthy? If the characters of the people concerned are such it may be more difficult to disbelieve them than to take into account phenomenon that appears to be of supernatural origin. Perhaps it is not supernatural, but rather profoundly natural, part of our universe and its order; but as yet our philosophy has not been able to encompass these experiences fully, or integrate them into our scientific framework of knowledge. The two forms of enquiry, the spiritual and the scientific, may not be in as much conflict as we think.

We know now that lack of love can affect the actual growth rate of the human body in a child. Lack of truth can distort and sicken the mind so that it destroys itself and sometimes its body or another's with its own destruction. Lack of justice creates bloody revolution. The great ethical imperatives that all the spiritual men and women down the ages have taught and lived are an integral power and force in our lives and circumstances . . . and whatever God is, He is about Life and Truth and Loving . . .

To know the one is to know the other.

Chapter 14

I work all day and get half drunk at night,
Waking at four to soundless dark, I stare.
In time the curtain-edges will grow light,
Till then I see what's really always there:
Unresting death, a whole day nearer now,
Making all thought impossible but how
And where and when I shall myself die,
Arid interrogation: yet the dread
Of dying, and being dead,
Flashes afresh to hold and horrify.

The mind blanks at the glare. Not in remorse
—The good not done, the love not given, time
Torn off unused . . .
But the total extinction that we travel to
And shall be lost in always. Not to be here,
Not to be anywhere,
And soon; nothing more terrible, nothing more true.

This is a special way of being afraid
No trick dispels. Religion used to try,
That vast moth-eaten musical brocade
Created to pretend we never die . . .

And so it stays just on the edge of vision,
A small unfocused blur, a standing chill

That slows each impulse down to indecision,
Most things may never happen: this one will,
And realisation of it rages out
In furnace-fear when we are caught without
People or drink. Courage is no good:
It means not scaring others. Being brave
Lets no one off the grave,
Death is no different whined at than withstood . . .

(Philip Larkin)

What a terrible poem. Yet we all know that fear, that question, that inevitability. Dylan Thomas said, 'Do not go gentle into that good night . . . rage, rage against the dying of the light . . .' But is death a dying of the light? There have been some who have said that the opposite may be more the case . . . that death is an entrance into light, into more light . . . lots and lots and lots of it . . . not an ending of life but rather a breaking of the bounds of the physical; a release of the spirit. Death now is the fulcrum point: the entrance–exit point.

What are we to make of Christ's claims to be a forerunner, going ahead to prepare a place for us? What of the clarion call of his apostle, Paul:

> But some will ask, 'How are the dead raised? With what kind of body do they come?' You foolish man! What you sow does not come to life unless it dies . . . So it is with the resurrection of the dead. What is sown is perishable, what is raised is imperishable . . . It is sown in weakness, it is raised in power. It is sown a physical body, it is raised a spiritual body. If there is a physical body, there is also a spiritual body. (1 Cor. 15:35-36, 42-44)

How did he know? How can we know? I wish I could be so sure. Is it a hope and a dream only or is it a reality given to a few to glimpse, so they can tell us of what is to come, so we who struggle after, along the shadowed way, might be comforted? Or are the great statements of the prophets and visionaries who claim to have seen something of the Celestial City, only a 'vast moth-eaten musical brocade/ Created to pretend we never die . . ?' It seems a little presumptuous to write off so many great men and women so . . . But how are we to know whether such things are illusion or an accurate report?

I want to know. I am not interested in illusion and fond hope; a hope that may cheer along the way but would disappear like a mirage at the grasp of a thirsty hand.

Perhaps those who do not believe might give an unbiased report, or at least one that does not come from their having been taught a belief system that was just assumed to be true. If someone was a frequent witness at the act of dying, that person might have learnt a thing or two about what it was about, from the outside of it at least.

I have a doctor aunt. My aunt was not only a doctor but a consultant pathologist. If anyone might know about dying, she might. She saw its effects every day as she searched for the pattern of cause and effect in illness and our body's ending. There was all that knowledge there. It seemed to me to be a shame not to use it in my search. Over twenty years later that conversation is etched in my mind as if on tablets of stone.

The words stand as reminders and signposts to a truth seen from the outside. In my travels both on the inner way and in the outer world I have had the chance to compare notes now and then with what was said so long ago. The correspondences are interesting.

Sitting on a sofa the colour of dried moss, waiting for the rain, I asked the question we will all ask one way or another . . . in the end.

'Aunt Ruth, do you believe in life after death? As a doctor, what do you think?'

My aunt looked very thoughtful. Then began my first lesson in the use of empirical observation. Science can perhaps take us some of the way on the metaphysical journey.

'You see,' she said, 'I have seen death many times. And there is this moment, this short period of time, when although the heart has stopped, the body is in full working order. There is enough oxygen in the blood stream for a few minutes to keep all the brain cells alive. This is why it is so necessary, if we are to resuscitate a patient to do it within this time, before the oxygen runs out and there is irreversible brain damage. During these four minutes *rigor mortis* has not begun, there are no essential changes that have taken place. If the patient is resuscitated all will be as before. But when you are there . . . at the moment of death, when the heart stops beating you can see a change . . . you can observe a difference that I cannot account for by any biochemical alteration in the body. There is no change in the body. The heart just happens to have stopped beating. You can get it going again but at that moment when the heart has stopped you see a change take place. The body becomes a thing. It begins to be a corpse . . . the person has gone. Whatever makes a body a person and not a thing goes. I don't know where it goes or how it comes back if you resuscitate the body but all I know is that that invisible thing, that I suppose in past ages was called a soul . . . goes . . . and we can get it back . . . sometimes. So yes . . . I believe in life after death . . . in some form . . . yes . . .'

There was a long silence. At this stage in my life I was not often silent.

I am a child of a scientific age. Empirical observation, which had led a non-religious person, trained to know and observe the body and all its functions so closely, to a metaphysical conclusion was convincing indeed. I was convinced. I still am.

Today I would approach the perimeter fence. Seven days had passed since I had sat by a bed and prayed to the silent air. Today I had been asked to see a body without life in it. What would it be like to see my grandmother dead?

Seven days . . . seven days . . . 'And on the seventh day God finished His work, which He had done and He rested on the seventh day from all His work which He had done. So God blessed the seventh day and hallowed it . . .'

. . . And on the seventh day my mother's mother rested from all her work that she had made. She rested from this life and was not . . . because God took her.

'Please, Sue, could you . . . could you come with me? The staff nurse said it might help . . . to see . . . to see . . .that it didn't help to run away from these things . . . that it might help . . . to see . . . to . . .'

'Yes, Mum, of course I'll come . . . It'll be all right . . .'

It was. But it wasn't easy. The deep things of life rarely are . . .

What would it be like? What would it be like to see the face and hands I had sat and drawn, as I struggled to catch the intricacy of the time-spider's-map over skin and bone and the black liveliness of the eyes within looking out? What would it be like?

But first there were the forms. There are always forms to be filled in around the edges of the most profound times . . . at birth and marriage and death. There are always the forms, the regulations: pieces of paper ushering us into the ante-room of the experience—the codifying and the attempt to control and categorise forces that are beyond us and yet within us—the tidal flow of the universe in its ebb and height, holding us and drawing us by a power beyond the Poles. And in its wake: the pathetic rags of paper.

The pieces of paper over and done with along with the statutory, friendly cup of tea, we were ushered across the red-waxed, quarry stone, gleaming floor to the closed door across the hall. On the other side of that door was the beginning of knowledge and the endings, the remnants of a life, the lees in the cup, that had been drunk to the bottom. It was a sight that I suspected I would never forget. I was right. I can see it now.

And 'it' was and is the right word to use. It was an 'it' and not a 'she'. There was no 'her' here. The person was not. She had gone. I knew it. For myself I knew. I had no need of philosophies or dogma. The matter was quite plain. The person I had known was not here. Here was only the cast-off skin . . .

'What dreams may come, when we have shuffled off this mortal coil . . .' Shakespeare knew all right. It was the cast-off skin that was left, with the bones giving an approximation of the lines and shape that the life had used to express itself.

What I hadn't expected was how small the body looked with the life left out. So small and sort of shrunken up; condensed and collapsed somehow around the gap that had been left. The face was terrible; a mask rather, a skull with skin covering it and a gaping mouth. But she wasn't there. This was what was left behind.

This small, shrunken thing lay stiffly under its stiff sheets on the high bed. We two, mother and daughter, stood in a silence thick with waiting: solid. And in that waiting and in that silence I knew that we were three. There was another who stood at our back. I saw nothing, heard nothing, but it was like something caught on the edge of vision but there, palpable.

It was a solidified stillness; a Presence centred in a core of quiet; it was . . . it was . . . there.

I cannot prove it. No instruments of this planet could catch and record its quality or dimension. But we know that there are entities beyond our human frame's possibility to experience. There are sounds that a dog can hear that are outside the range of the ears of its master. (So much for human superiority . . . in relation to consciousness maybe; in relation to the ears . . . definitely not!) There are light rays that are beyond our eyes' capacity to see. Now we have made machines that can show us these wonders but they were there before we knew it, waiting for us to discover them.

In the end all I can say is that I know. It was there, except that it was not an 'it'. We were not alone. In every sense of that word I knew ourselves not alone. I have known that presence twice since. The third time was also a kind of dying, but not of the body. But that was not yet, not for a long while yet. This was the first.

Chapter 15

'I have dreamed dreams that have gone through and through me and changed the colour of my mind . . .' So says Catherine Earnshaw in *Wuthering Heights*, talking to her nurse and confidante Nelly Dean.

Are dreams just phantoms—a jumbled jangle of images—a result of a computer-sort-out of data, whilst the machine of the mind was 'off-line', as was suggested recently by a BBC programme looking at the phenomena of dreams? This theory may have some truth but not, I suspect, all of it. Our culture is not well practised at discerning the different qualities and levels of the dream experience.

Yet through the ages, in many other cultures as well as in our own past, has come the teaching that the dream experience can at times be the mode through which spiritual knowledge and experience can come to us.

But as in all learning we have to be ready for the next stage and be able to regard the experiences that come to us as both useful and reliable if we are to gain from what they have to teach us. As in all other areas of human life some have a greater capacity and sensitivity than others, whether it is for the harmonising of colour or sounds, the making of stories, or the capacity to dream true dreams . . .

In Africa the wise men and women and witch-doctors of the tribe were partly chosen, so Jung tells us, for their ability to dream true dreams—the Big Dreams that would help and save and strengthen both the individual and the tribe. With the coming of the white settlers with their western, materialistic, scientific view of the world, the blacks gave up their trust in the 'Dream Time', as the Aborigine would say, and with the dying of this trust, so the dreams died too, withering away into only a memory. In darkening times we need to learn to dream again.

> And it shall come to pass afterward,
> that I will pour out my spirit on all flesh;
> your sons and your daughters shall prophesy,
> your old men shall dream dreams,
> and your young men shall see visions.
> Even upon the menservants and maidservants
> in those days I will pour out my spirit. (Joel 2: 28–29)

Dream, vision and prophesy are linked together. In all three the power and mystery of symbols are evoked to lead the mind to truths that lie beyond the surface of what we know and experience in everyday reality. Jung describes symbols and their ability to provoke a response in us as being different in kind to either an allegory or sign, being 'an image which describes in the best possible way the dimly discerned nature of the spirit. A symbol does not define or explain; it points beyond itself to a meaning that is darkly divined but is still beyond our grasp and cannot be adequately expressed in the familiar words of our language.'

In the dream we are between the conscious and the unconscious, between sleeping and waking. It is perhaps this intermediacy that facilitates the possibility of breakthrough into a different level of consciousness.

Recent research into the phenomenon called Lucid Dreaming, in which dreamers are aware that they dream and can influence the course of their dream as well as signalling to an outside observer in a sleep laboratory that they are aware and dreaming, has shown that consciousness and unconscious material can interrelate. The researchers also found that the body, although to all intents and purposes in a paralysed state, echoes in itself the movements of the body of the dreamers in their dreams. It seems that what is done in the body affects the mind and the nature of the dream, and what is done in the dream affects the body. We are what we do and what we do affects what we are.

At the end of a programme on Lucid Dreaming on BBC's 'Everyman' series (Nov. 1985), three lucid dreamers decided on an experiment. They would agree to meet during a lucid dream at a particular place and, if it were possible, they would recount what had happened there to each other the next day on waking. Two of the three dreamed in a way in which they were conscious and they were able to meet in their dream at the designated place: a park known to them. In the park they had a conversation, part of which notes the absence of the third friend. When the three friends met the next day, they compared notes. One had been absent, because he had not dreamed consciously that night. The other two both remembered their dream and found it corresponded exactly. They had both gone to the park in their dream as arranged and found that what they remembered and experienced corresponded precisely. It was a remarkable synchronising of experience, carried out consciously and by choice. It appears that we are more interrelated than we think and that our thoughts and intentions can unite us, crossing time and space.

The experiences of these two men have some interesting correspondences with, and also some fascinating differences from dream experiences that occurred when I and some close friends made our first tentative steps of exploration into areas outside the more well-travelled paths described by the church I had entered. In the beginning you could say that this area of the dream experience bumped into us rather than vice versa but once begun, the questions and implications flowed in like a tidal current.

I believe that in the spiritual life, there is room for reverent experiment. It is a mode by which we learn and check our experience and conclusions in other areas of life, so why not in this? It is a new territory, whose boundaries, forms and nature have to be learnt about, discovered, walked in and then stood back from so that the overall pattern can be discerned.

* * *

On the eve of manhood, Joseph dreamed two dreams. He was a young man and not wise in the ways of the world, but what can you expect from a seventeen-year-old? His favoured position as the child of his father's old age did not incline him to have an old head on his young shoulders. If he had been wise he would have kept his mouth shut. But if he had known wisdom ahead of his time and kept silence, the pattern would not have sent him to Egypt.

In the exile and in the pain came the redemption. It is often so . . .

The redemption came for him and for all his clan and even beyond the clan for the people who, to avoid death, went into exile. Redemption came by one man, through the one man who had been a slave and learnt patience and humility in a jail. So even in the foolishness and ignorance of the unaware, the spirit of God moves still, to fulfil in us the pattern of our destiny. For some, in the individual finding and acceptance of their pattern, is woven the pattern and place of many. And so it was with this man.

Was the meaning of the pictures in Joseph's dream obscure, needing interpretation? The dream of the young Joseph spoke in symbols, yes, but as traditional Jewish wisdom notes, 'the dream is its own interpretation'. The meaning in this case of sheaves of corn bowing down to Joseph's sheaf was quite obvious to his brothers. They were none too pleased about it. The second dream was no better than the first, adding insult to injury even. The sun and moon and eleven stars bowed down to Joseph. The meaning was obvious, arrogantly, irritatingly obvious and his father knew it. 'His father rebuked him, and said to him, "What is this dream that you have dreamed? Shall I and your mother and your brothers indeed come to bow ourselves to the ground before you?" And his brothers were jealous of him, but his father kept the saying in mind.' (Gen. 3: 10–11)

His brothers had every reason to be jealous of this favoured child of their father. I suspect he was insufferable. But when it came to the crunch, when their young brother's life hung by a thread, two brothers spoke for the saving of a life. They were listened to, and saved their brother Joseph from death; so powerful can a word be. And in that speaking they saved their brothers from a corporate act of murder and fratricide. And in their words of mercy, mercy was given to them. Their word saved a life and in that saving was their own and all their family's. Not that they knew it then.

'Blessed are the merciful for they shall obtain mercy.'

The dreams in fact were true, but the way to the fulfilment of the dreams was not told . . . and a good thing too!

Was the dream a night time daydream? Was it a desire for power that would have satisfied the theories of Adler? Who can say and how do we know? Perhaps the clue is only in the consciousness of the dreamer. Jung insisted that in the interpretation of any dream, there was no rigid system whereby one symbol always carried a particular meaning. Any possible dream interpretation had to have accord within the mind and inner self of the dreamer; only then could one safely say the meaning had been found. To Joseph, this dream was particularly worth the telling. Perhaps it felt different from the other kind. The family themselves accepted its possible prophetic import much as they disliked it.

That was then and this is now. But the need to tell the difference between the two kinds of dream is still with us. On the spiritual way, the need may become an imperative. In the long years of slavery and unjust imprisonment I suspect Joseph thought long and hard on just this question. For the while, nothing seemed farther from the truth than his dream.

And to his prison came the butler and the baker of the king of Egypt. And one night they both dreamed, the butler and the baker, 'each his own dream and each dream with its own meaning'.

Joseph had learnt a little compassion in the troubles of his way. Seeing the worried faces of the two men, he asked them why they were downcast? He found they too had had dreams that they suspected were significant, but they did not know the meaning of them.

Joseph said to them, 'Do not interpretations belong to God? Tell them to me, I pray you.'

How did he know that he would be given the meaning, that he would know? I do not know . . . but he knew and in his knowing was the beginning of his release and of the saving that was to come. But the beginning of the ending, that was also in a much deeper way a beginning of the situation foretold in the dreams of his youth, was to last two years. There are seven hundred and thirty days in two years. In prison the days are full of hours. It was a long time to wait.

A year went by and then another. Unknown to the man still in prison, the king dreamed a dream and when he woke it was not like at other times. His spirit was troubled. All the wise men were asked the meaning of the dream but they could not interpret it. He knew, somehow that this dream was not to be ignored, that help was needed. It seemed that he knew that this dream, and its repetition in slightly different form, was significant. And then the butler remembered the Hebrew who had helped him, whom he had forgotten in the joy of his release and in the consequent ending of his own need. So Joseph was brought out of prison. When the king told him that he had heard that Joseph could interpret dreams, the prisoner corrected him:

'It is not in me; God will give Pharaoh a favourable answer.' And having heard the two dreams, Joseph said to Pharaoh, 'The dream of Pharaoh is one; God has revealed to Pharaoh what he is about to do.'

Mind you, the answer wasn't too comforting. However the king got what he needed—the answer to his dream, which was also what the man needed in his role as protector of the people and ruler of the realm. He was told what was to come, 'and the doubling of the dream means that the thing is fixed by God and God will shortly bring it to pass.'

One could logically infer that if the doubling means that something is fixed, then one incident of a dream of warning could mean that the events foreseen are a possibility. That there is still room for manoeuvre, that there is a space and flexibility of the pattern in that area and time.

So the dream became a preparation so that suffering could be alleviated. But to turn the warning into preparation needed a human response of imagination and structuring and discipline. Interestingly, Joseph had learned the lessons of waiting well. He did not presume that the man to deal with the problem would be him. It had taken thirteen years of suffering to free Joseph from the need to be a leader, to be important. Although a slave, he was in a deeper sense truly a free man and the Pharaoh knew it, recognising the wisdom with which the man who was outwardly a slave spoke. Being free of the need for power, Joseph was given power. Being content to be just a man who listened to the voice of God if he was given that opportunity, so that he might help others along their way, he was given the status and the position that he no longer assumed nor sought. In the understanding of the dream of warning, his own dream of foretelling of the pattern of his life was fulfilled. The fulfilment was, it seems, contingent on an act of kindness. In seeing the troubled faces of the fellow prisoners two years previously Joseph could have been so enclosed by his own suffering tht he ignored theirs. In his compassion was the seed of his own freedom.

From the dream to the reality of which it spoke was thirteen years. This was only the beginning of the coming of his dreams. The seven years of plenty passed and in the second set of seven the dreams were fully realised. Twenty-one years or more: the years for the making of a man. It had been a long time but perhaps worth the waiting.

* * *

I have not dreamed big dreams like that. In a small life one must begin small. And anyway who is to say which is small and which is big? I get less interested in deciding which is which. I suspect only God and Time will tell us. And maybe the question in eternity has no importance. It is not size but quality, I suspect, that counts in the end.

At a similar age to Joseph when he began to dream I began to read this book of books and in it I noticed that He who was called God could speak through dreams . . . so if then, then why not now and if them . . . why not me? Human beings then could not be so different . . . 'If you prick us, do we not bleed . . . if you tickle us, do we not laugh?' In the asking was the beginning of the answering. As with other matters on the road to the Celestial City, the answering was not in the way I had expected. But I was glad when it came.

With the coming of this dream, this small dream that yet pointed to something larger than itself, came hope. And I was in great need of hope. The dream spoke of connections beyond the separateness of our bodies. It showed me the reality of what John Donne wrote, that no man is an island, entire of itself. It was my first lesson and demonstration of the fact that we all may be members of one another.

'As for prophecies, they shall pass away . . . as for knowledge, it shall pass away . . . so faith, hope and love abide, these three . . .'

It was certainly a surprise, this dream: for the dreamer and for me. It has changed us both. It was a beginning.

So what was this little dream? Little it was in its actual picture and duration but the implications are not, I think, little. But for that you must judge for yourself.

When I was twenty the world went grey. The mid-year blues common to students mid-way through their course turned black indeed. I didn't know why, not then. It was just so.

O the mind, mind has mountains; cliffs of fall
Frightful, sheer no-man-fathomed. Hold them cheap
May who ne'er hung there . . .
. . . Here! creep,
Wretch, under a comfort serves in a whirlwind: all
Life death does end and each day dies with sleep.

(Gerard Manley Hopkins)

I read these words as part of my studies. I read them again and again and again. Thank God! Someone had said it! Someone had felt exactly the same: had caught the inexpressible in words. Oh, the relief of it!

My church and Christian friends did not approve of my

attempts to say how it was within the inner world. The truth does not always fit in with one's philosophy. I was exhorted to pray more, read my Bible more, go to church more. I tried to follow their advice. It was an abysmal failure. The heavens were as brass and I grew only in cynicism. I became an embarrassment. Not for the first time, nor I suspect for the last.

The greyness within and without grew colder, the despair ever nearer. What would become of me? Was I completely forgotten, the heavens silent, the gates barred and bolted?

'Have mercy, Oh Christ in heaven, have mercy. Hear my prayer. If you who are, can hear my prayer, have mercy. Somehow, somehow let me know I am not alone, forsaken on this whirling planet, a speck amongst the circling stars, without meaning, without purpose, without hope . . . If beyond my thought somehow, someone hears . . . if it matters at all . . . may I know it. May I know myself not forsaken, not ultimately alone.'

I did not know it then but was to know it later, that I was indeed answered. As in all the best science fiction, messages that come from the stars, travelling even at the speed of light, when they reach the dust of this dark yet glorious planet, take a little time to get through to us.

Unknown to me at the time, a young woman in my home city dreamed a dream.

We had met briefly, talked of politics and music. I remember she had worn a Marimekko dress: an unusual Finnish print. I had been a small part of her journey into faith. Then we had gone our separate ways, or so we thought.

And in that other city, another body dreamed the dream that was to be dreamt. In the dream this woman saw a girl slumped over a desk and knew the figure that she saw was me. And in the dream was a knowing. The body that she saw told her that I despaired, although no word was said.

The woman whom I had known a little awoke and knew this dream was different. This was not like the dreams she had dreamed before. This dream was a call and a knowing for a purpose.

But nothing is beyond doubt and she, like I, was not used to these things. So this woman on the beginning of the Way prayed for wisdom and understanding. In the midst of the prayer the vision of the dream was known to be a call; a call to go and visit the other who was nearly a stranger; a call to just . . . be there.

'But she didn't know. It was only a dream when all was said and done. It was perhaps just one of those odd things in life. You couldn't travel from one city to another on the strength of a dream, now could you? What a fool you'd look knocking at the door and saying a dream had sent you. You couldn't do that, could you? This was the twentieth century. It was absurd, quite absurd.'

And so this woman at the beginning of her Way tempted Fate, but Fate for the while was quite happy to be tempted.

'I will open the Bible,' said the young woman to the silent heavens. 'I will open the Bible and whatever my eye looks at, that will be what I have to do. Now I can't be told to go and travel to Leeds from the Bible, can I?'

With a grin and a shrug and yet an inward wonder, the girl opened this most dangerous of books and the dice having been thrown, Fate with a smile threw it back. The eyes of a young woman looked with horror and laughter at the page open on her lap. Her eye had caught the words from the book of Jonah:

'Go, get ye up and go to that great city . . .'

It doesn't do to throw the gauntlet at God; He just might throw it back at your feet and then you're in for it.

And so the answer to my prayer got on to a train and in the fullness of time arrived at my door. Poor woman—she wasn't exactly welcomed with open arms.

Chapter 16

The door bell rang. I opened the door. There she stood. Why on earth was she here? I did *not* feel like small talk.

There was a small silence.

The smile on the other's face wobbled a bit uncertainly.

'What on earth are you doing here?' I said. Not a promising beginning.

'Can I come in?' she said.

'If you like.'

She followed me down to the subterranean living room of the flat. The polite cups of coffee half finished, there was another small silence in which I could see her reaching for the right words to break the tension, like someone fumbling in a handbag to find a precious purse. I did not help her.

'Are you all right?' she said.

I looked at her. She looked at me.

'No. No, I'm not.'

There was a longer silence. How much would it be worth saying to this apparently caring stranger, whom I had known so little. The silence stretched itself around us while I considered the risk of speaking how it was.

'Why do you ask?'

This time it was the other who waited as I fumbled around inside the darkness of my mind, wondering what, if anything, to say. She did not reply . . . just waited, which was in itself a sort of response. Perhaps this time someone actually wanted to know. And so I told her, bitterly and angrily; the barbed-wire-words falling between us:

'These Christians . . . they make me sick! I'm sick of them and their sugar smiles. "You can smile and smile and be a villain . . ." I'm sick of the whole pack of them! Them and their smiley words. They haven't a clue. I could wrap them in a reef-knot around a lamp post. All they do is give me sermons and they're not even vicars! But, my God, they sound like it! And it doesn't work . . . what they say . . . and . . . and I feel so cut off . . . and they talk of this "relationship with God" and all that stuff and I don't know what they are talking about . . . and . . . and . . . it's like the world's gone grey . . . inside and out . . . and it's such a relief just to go to sleep and not be aware for a bit . . . and when I pray . . . all I do is cry and I don't know what on earth I'm crying about . . . And I haven't cried for years and I didn't intend to start now, particularly if I don't know what I'm crying about . . . Oh, and what's the use of anything . . . and . . . sometimes I think I'm going mad . . .'

Still the woman opposite was silent. The Christians I knew were hardly ever silent.

Somehow the silence was an encouragement.

In the silence I thought of the words of Gerard Manley Hopkins. He'd said it like it was . . .

Here! Creep,
Wretch, under a comfort serves in a whirlwind: all
Life death does end and each day dies with sleep.

It was as if she had heard it and knew . . .

'I don't know what to say . . . I haven't experienced what you are saying. But I want you to know why I came . . .'

And she told me. Then she went. That was all.

It was enough.

A small miracle can go a long way. It lasted me for months: a bulwark against despair. Twenty years on I remember and am thankful. It was a beginning of a different road for both of us. That dream and its meaning for me changed us both. It began a search that led us beyond itself. In different ways we had asked something of the heavens and we were answered. We are not the same people that we were.

I'm glad that Job wasn't indicted for his arguments and protestations. His pious friends were, however. His religious friends who tried to sort out the messy, painfilled tangle of life into a neat, codified, systematic arrangement, in which the innocent escaped and only the guilty suffered, were the ones who were condemned. My head has been full of arguments and disputations for the last twenty years. Sometimes there are areas of quiet when my philosophy and experience are of a piece, then the next wave has arrived from the inner or outer horizon and I'm spluttering again with my head just above or just below the water-line wondering whether I will ever get to firm land again. Perhaps I'd better learn to swim instead!

I suspect that swimming will entail being able to keep my head above water, when I'm out of my depth and that skill and confidence will take me to a place beyond the inner arguments, divisions and disputations . . .

*   *   *

Slowly but surely over painfilled months I came to the conclusion that my raging against the silent heavens was misdirected. Perhaps the problem resided *in* me, as opposed to in a divinity that seemed so withdrawn. In the quiet that can come at the end of weeping I began to see that perhaps the gap, the sense of separation and desolation, were factors of my inner universe that needed recognition. In a while the gap began to be filled. But the dark thread of that recognition is with me still, and what began in the beginnings of resolution at university gave me a breathing space to grow in strength awhile, so that in time, when the time was right a deeper knowing and a deeper learning and change could take place. The beginning was a willingness to encounter the Divine Other, in ways that went beyond my rational understanding as it was at that time. The wisdom of God is indeed open to reason, but the reasoning it is open to may operate from different premises to the ones you currently hold.

It was my turn now. I had been on the receiving end of a dream that spoke of interrelationship and a connectedness within human, spiritual consciousness. It was my turn next to be at the other end of this new possibility of the dreaming mode of experience. It was all so simple, so small, so eminently easy to miss.

The grasping of its significance was in fact dependent at the time, unused as I was to these things, on a sense of humour and an ironic amusement with myself.

One night I dreamed a dream and knew I dreamed. It was as straightforward as if I were watching a video. I was an unseen observer, aware that I observed. What did I see? Only a simple ordinary thing. A friend walking down the road, hand in hand with her man. I knew them both but believed that they were not connected, that in fact my friend had been deeply troubled by the question of commitment in a relationship with a different boy. I laughed at myself ruefully and wondered whether the spring was getting to my brain! Why on earth had I seen these two together of all things? Puzzled and amused I went off for a day's study.

Accidentally or 'coincidentally', I happened to meet my friend on the campus. We did not normally meet on such a day and time. We went for coffee and talked of this and that and the other . . . of nothing much, and then on a whim, to amuse my friend, I said, 'Guess what! I had such a funny dream last night! You won't half laugh!' I was in the middle of the story and so did not notice my friend's sudden stillness. The story ended. I wondered why she sat so still and white. There was a tiny pause and then the subject was hurriedly changed. Oh dear, I thought, I've made a bit of a clanger there. Oh, well . . .

Later, many weeks later, I heard the other half of the story.

In much agony of spirit, my friend, having had two serious relationships that had become tangled and painful, had prayed to know whether this third man who had begun to move on to her inner horizon was the one that was meant as part of her pattern, whether this time this relationship would have life in it and would be a choosing that would be pleasing to God.

Can we ask such questions? Are they a reflection of our need and longing for guidance and comfort in the tangles and fogginess of life; only a sign of our immaturity and insecurity? Well . . . if God is . . . if there is an intelligence that has personality, that is involved in humankind, both within and without . . . then why not? Still, it was worth a try and if you do not ask, you can never know. It is only in the asking and the questing, in the searching and the doing that we begin to see shadows of patterns, glimmerings of truth that tell that we might not be alone in our voyage through time.

Abraham's servant was shown by God the girl who was to be Isaac's wife. It is interesting how the servant set up the boundaries of the experiment. He prayed that the girl who went the 'second mile', the one who would be generous in spirit, kind to the man and his animals, 'let her be the one whom thou has appointed for thy servant Isaac. By this I shall know that thou has shown steadfast love to my master' (Gen. 24:14) His wisdom was responded to.

My friend, for reasons unknown to me, asked to be shown

in a dream. Dreams cannot be had to order. They are 'given' things. That night she slept and remembered nothing. That night, I was later to learn, was the night I saw my friend hand in hand with the man who was obviously on the way to being the lover and the husband he was to become.

On its own such a little, little thing. In the context of the prayer and the asking; in the context of the meeting and the telling; in the context of my complete ignorance of the prayer or of the man and his relationship with her or why such a dream should be necessary; this little, little thing, spoke louder than itself.

'No man is an Island, entire of itself; every man is a piece of the Continent, a part of the main.' (John Donne)

There is a strong tradition of those who struggle to find the way of God having to be willing to walk the way of the Fool . . . but who is mad and who is sane? Who is the King and who is the Fool in *King Lear*?

It is only back-ends-on that we can see the divine wisdom in the Fool and the willingness to be a Fool, in the mercy and kindness that is also in what we give the name God . . .

My friend had prayed that she would be shown in a dream. At the forking of the ways and at a time of choosing, like Gideon she asked for a sign from the heavens as to where on the road the 'good' lay. She was open to either possibility. She was not fixed in her will and intent, but flexible of heart, ready to move forward or back. The sign was given. She asked for it to come in a dream and in a dream it came. The asking and the response were linked exactly in time. It was just the agent that was changed.

The dream was given to another and yet the knowledge of the dream came to her as she needed and had asked. In the difference and in the change was, I think, a marked and important alteration. If she had been given exactly what she wanted, a dream that indicated 'this is the man', always after she could have argued in herself that her own desires had created the dream, that it was only a wish-fufilment after all. As a sign and indication of possibilities that were pleasing to the divine mind, it would have been useless. But the dream was 'given' or rather arrived in the consciousness of a sleeper who was connected to her who prayed by friendship but in nothing else. I knew nothing of the need, the situation or the prayer and in that was some objectivity. And in that separation, the dream assumed the stature, little though it was, of the sign that was needed.

In little ways I had begun to learn of new possibilities of mind and spirit. Nothing is ever wasted. There is, I think, a divine economy and super efficiency in the divine mind. Experiences of the spirit seem to have within them many layers of meaning and possibilities. It wasn't long after the expanding of my understanding of the dream experience, that I had great need of the little I had begun to learn.

There are many instances in the biblical accounts of dreams and visions, of them being used to help, prepare and forewarn the people of God of what lay ahead, either for the individual or for the group of which they were a part. What is frustratingly absent is any means by which we are helped to discern the difference between genuine dreams of forewarning and guidance and mere projections of our own fears.

Abraham, in a vision of the night that was no easy, pleasant thing, was told of the coming slavery of his people, which was to last for four hundred years. But he was told that he would live to an old age and die in peace.

Nebuchadnezzar asked his wise men not only to tell him the meaning of his dream, but to tell him what he had dreamed that night. Quite a tall order, even with the concentrating power of a death penalty hanging over you for failure! When Daniel had accomplished this astonishing feat, (a living evidence that there was a God in Heaven who revealed mysteries, having being given the meaning himself through a vision of the night), the king dreamed for a second time. This time the dream was not to make known to the king 'what shall be hereafter,' but was rather a warning against his spiralling pride. The king did not heed the warning and lost his likeness to both God and man and became as a beast, as was foretold in his dream.

But . . . but . . . how do you know . . .?

It was not easy then. It is not easy now . . .

So at the beginning of the way I was moved towards deeper waters.

One week in my final year at university, I dreamed two dreams.

The first dream was small, simple and ordinary but so real and normal that the dividing line between reality and the dream was nearly broken. I lay in bed and heard the telephone ring. I heard the footsteps of someone coming up to my room to wake me. Then sleepily I went downstairs to answer the phone, to hear a nurse from a hospital say that my mother needed me and could I come as soon as was possible . . .

I woke listening for the phone. It did not ring . . . not then . . .

But . . . but surely, surely this was just fear, unconscious fear that had surfaced in the dream. I knew my mother was not well and lived alone. But I had prayed that if ever I should be needed, somehow He who was and knew all things would make sure I was where I was needed. But the dream was no doubt an expression of a fear . . . no more . . .

Finals were only weeks away. I dismissed the nagging doubt. I was a modern woman, intelligent, rational; such a dream was clearly a crystallisation of my fear, nothing more . . . surely. But I could not forget it, try as I might. It stayed in the back of my mind while I carried on ignoring it.

The next experience was neither simple nor ordinary, and was not to be ignored. It would have been possible to dismiss it. But I recognised that this was Other . . . this was different; this was of another quality and needed my full attention.

I was in a state caught between sleeping and waking. I was aware of my body at rest in its bed, my eyes closed and yet I was aware. A presence stood by my bed and spoke. I could not see it. But it was there, palpable, standing at an exact point: to the left of my shoulder.

Words were spoken to my mind. My mother would be in danger of death in six days. Then the scene changed and I was there. I saw my mother. I saw my body standing at a certain place in the room. I heard myself speak. There was no fear. It would be an ending which was also a beginning. I saw and knew more but the specific details are for her and me to discover in time and in the hidden God who unites us all.

But what of the present? I knew that time was always problematic in these things. I had read enough to know that. Was this sort of thing to be relied on, acted on? I knew the meaning of the phrase, 'Pharaoh woke and was troubled in spirit'.

I prayed for wisdom. The first lecture that day was on Chaucer and had been rearranged due to a cancellation. It was all about people being warned of a hidden truth in a dream! I did not feel like a cup of coffee afterwards . . . a brandy would have been more appropriate.

Two days later my mother phoned and said . . . not to worry, but she had to go into hospital for tests and that she'd had a 'little do' . . . and could not go on holiday as planned. It was enough. I would go home and be there . . . just in case . . .

It would do no harm to go home for the weekend, even with Finals three weeks away. There was a slight hitch; the sixth day was on the Monday. Just to be on the safe side, I asked the professor and the warden of the hall of residence for permission 'if it was needed', to be away for another day or two.

I said nothing of the dream. I was a twentieth century girl. I was used to the ways of reason. And using that reason it was sensible to go in the light of the given evidence, both outside and in . . . after all, you never know . . . better safe than sorry . . .

I stayed the extra day. Feeling like a fool I spoke to the sister in charge of the ward. 'Oh, by the way . . . should there be any emergency . . . I'm not staying at home, perhaps you had better have my number.'

The starched face looked with resigned patience at what it obviously regarded as a neurotic student.

'That will be quite unnecessary. Your mother is only in for tests . . . and is doing very well. There is no cause for alarm . . .'

With the vision at my back I ploughed awkwardly on. 'Still, you never know, do you? You might as well take it down . . . just in case,' I said. 'You never know, do you?'

I bid farewell to my mother, resplendent in new-for-the-hospital pink bed-jacket. She certainly looked fine.

Berating myself as a gullible, idiotic fool, I went down the interminable hospital corridors. I walked and bussed my weary and worried way back to my godmother's house. But deep down inside I knew.

As I opened the door the telephone rang.

I was not surprised.

It was the hospital. My mother had had a heart attack. Could I inform the next of kin, and when we came to see her we must only stay for two to three minutes at the most.

My brother at my side, I returned to the hospital room I had so recently left. It was the sixth day. I have never seen a face that had altered so drastically, so fast, the skin chalk and paper white; the eye-sockets black holes in space, sunken back in the skull. It did not look like the mother we knew. She could not speak. I sat and held her hand. It seemed the only thing to do.

The statutory few minutes over, we left the room. My poor brother was more shocked than I, but the change, the change in that face silenced us both.

The heels of our shoes went clacketty-clack on the hard, orderly, black tarmac of the car-park.

'She doesn't look too good, does she?' said my brother, frowning carefully down his nose.

In his twenty-five years of English life, my brother had certainly mastered the art of the understatement, a skill I took much longer to appreciate.

I had prayed that He who was the Prime Mover would move me to where I was needed. Without the dream/vision, just before the Final examinations I would not have come home.

Within six days of earth time my mother nearly died. Six is an interesting number according to Jewish mystical teaching. It is the number of incompletion. This part of the story, like all the stories of the living while they live, is incomplete. It is not an incompletion that I mind.

Twice I had come near to the perimeter fence, to the outskirts of mortality. The third time was not what I expected but it was, on due reflection most appropriate. The third time I approached the border country was at a birth . . .

Chapter 17

What does it mean to become a parent? The answer would appear to be obvious. To become a parent is to have a child: to create a family. We do not always know what we do. We who are the children become the parents. We, who had someone ahead of us, in time if in nothing else, move into the front line. In becoming parents, no matter what the route, we set off a depth charge that one way or another will alter us.

For those who make a conscious choice to lend their bodies for the creation of life, the act is known as one of the few irrevocable acts we do and know that we do. We know that we will be changed by it, for better or for worse till the end of time. Perhaps in all acts we are changed by the action no matter how small, but in this act we are aware we are changed and will be changed and have wrought a great change in life's pattern: a new life that was not, now is . . .

Biology may or may not be destiny but certainly a woman's body teaches her that a time can come when time begins to run out, that choices are not always deferable.

The time came for me when I had to choose. I was in my early thirties and in the fifth year of my marriage. I have learnt since that Jewish tradition links meaning with number . . . and five is associated with the themes of division and creation. In the fifth year of my marriage a process of division and creation began. As with so many other things it was not quite what I expected.

There was a call within the core of myself and experienced within my body in a way that I had never known before. Deep within the silence that is at the centre of the self I knew it was time . . .

Within the flesh and matter that was I, it spoke. 'Now is the time,' it said. 'Now . . . for you . . . it is now. You need to decide now.'

I chose and I chose freely. In this choosing that went beyond rationality, there was no sense of compulsion. I was free, free utterly to decide. I was just being warned that the time was running out. I had thought that that sense had derived from the physical urgency of the body. Now, I suspect that in some deep sense I was warned that in other ways that were hidden from me the time for the possibility of a child was running out.

The time of choice was now; the eternal now; the now of over seven years ago. Interesting that that time of choice should come after seven years of knowing my man. Seven . . . the number of completion; something was finished and the next phase of a new beginning was at the door waiting.

I know that for myself; I did not feel free or at ease consciously to choose childlessness. If it happened, if that was the way of it, that was a different matter. But to choose it for me . . . for me alone and for no other, I knew would be to choose a sterile path. We can only choose for ourselves, listen to the mystery that is in the silence at the centre and say 'yes' or 'no' to the question that is put to us there.

I asked my man what he thought. What did *he* want? He was quiet . . . didn't look at me, I remember now . . . and said, yes, he would like a child . . .

Life, in some ways is just. Later, much later, he told me that he had thought that having a child would 'help'. I had not known that we needed that sort of 'help'.

Children come with their own call, their own challenge, their own pain. They need all the help they can get, when they come, 'crying that they come to this great stage of fools . . .'. They do not bring us 'help'. They do come with gifts in those curling and uncurling flesh-flower-hands. They can bring us wisdom and a new discovery of the simple things of life; a discovery of a different time-scale and maybe a discovery of a different continent within. I was given that being, spun from my flesh. I rear my son as I discovered I truly chose him: alone.

* * *

I come from a culture that loves marriage. It is at the heart of the faith. The Jews, exiles within the world, found until recently their centre within the home, within the family, wherever they happened to be. And at the heart of the centre is the mother; the Jewish Mother: the pivot point on which the harmony of the home rests.

Carl Jung makes some interesting comments on the depths and resonances within the terrible and awesome symbol that is the word 'Mother'.

> This is the mother-love, which is one of the most moving and unforgettable memories of our lives, the mysterious root of all growth and change; the love that means homecoming, shelter and the long silence from which everything begins and in which everything ends . . . Mother is mother-love, my experience and my secret. Why risk saying too much, too much that is false and inadequate and beside the point, about that human being who was our mother; the accidental carrier of that great experience, which includes herself and myself and all mankind, and indeed the whole of created nature, the experience of life whose children we are? . . . but a sensitive person cannot in all fairness load that enormous burden of meaning, responsibility, duty, heaven and hell,

onto the shoulders of one frail and fallible human being—so deserving of love, understanding—who was our mother. (*Psychological Reflections*)

Sometimes another culture or faith can perceive a truth that we are too close to, too involved in, to perceive the pattern that is forming. And in all patterns there are the gaps: the silences.

For the Jew, or so it was, the married man was the complete man and children add to his blessings. Not for them the sideways glance, the nudge and wink and look of sorrowful commiseration, the bitter jests about the loss of freedom and the coming of imprisonment at the approach of their marriage.

I was appalled at the jokes of my husband's English male friends on our engagement. I was appalled and hurt. There's many a truth told in jest, so they say. We should look most carefully at what those barbed words with their laughing masks tell us. In my race, such jokes are seldom made.

Whenever I met a Jewish woman friend of my mother's, she would look at me with a smile of hope in her eyes. Then the eyebrows would lift in a question to me and to my mother . . . 'Your daughter, she is married?'

'Yes,' I would reply, 'I'm married.'

'That is good, yes . . .' The eyes of my mother's friend would glint and sparkle, a sun-specks-dance. 'You have . . . children . . . yes?'

'Not yet,' I would say . . .

The eyes-light would fade; the voice drop as before a death. Then the voice would lift again . . .

'Still . . . soon . . . yes? You will have children?'

'Yes, maybe . . . in time . . . We will perhaps have children . . .'

My heart warmed to that sun-spark glint. It was like the

gleam and delicate wonder of blossom in the spring; a herald to the magic of new life come again. I had not realised how much I had missed it, that sparkle in the eyes, or how barren was my heart remembering the jests of my husband's friends at another's wedding and the young men's voices ringing in my ears: 'We'll buy you a ball and chain for your wedding present.' Was I supposed to laugh? I didn't and my face was as cold as my heart. My husband's shoulders shrugged aside the jibe, but no word was spoken against it. They say that in court silence is construed as consent. I should have been warned.

The Jewish people believe in marriage. And within the marriage is the child that is looked for: the essence of what is between man and woman; the power to create life; a new living being. In the Jewish way, children are a part of being married; they go together with it like fish and chips or strawberries and cream and bread and butter. It is not that they must come, or that the physical union is only sacred and allowed if it creates their passage, as seems to be the case at times in the teachings of the celibate priests of the Roman Church, but rather that children are a gift of life, to be treasured and enjoyed, whilst our guardianship of them lasts.

Our society gives lip-service to the honour and importance of parenthood. But in the big, national companies, do the executives concern themselves with the effects on wife and children of that much-vaunted mobility they demand in their aspiring young men? They move them round the country, filling approprite slots in the financial chess game; the young men thinking they will become bishop or castle, when in reality they are just the pawns of administrative neatness and company convenience. Ambition and work are to be one's honour and goal; not children.

And for the single mother and the woman in the high-rise

flat with nowhere to dry the clothes and nowhere for her children to play, where is this much vaunted concern? Nor do you see young children in the restaurants at the dinner parties of those who can afford to eat out. They are there, the children, in Italy, and in France and in Greece . . . but here?

And the Church with all its Family Services and its Sunday schools? Do they run the Family Crisis lines? Who has been in the forefront of endeavouring to help the women who fall into clinical depression after having a child? I do not see the Church as leaders and initiators in this work. At times it is interesting to see what is left out.

One in five women will suffer from post-natal depression after birth and those are the ones that are noticed, when something is very obviously going wrong. One in five hundred women will lose contact with the reality that we know and have a period of what is known as 'post-puerperal psychosis'. It is quite a costly business to bear another life, costly for the mind as well as the body.

If the woman begins to falter, very often the marriage, into which the child has come with so much need of love and help, begins to stagger and fall.

We all need someone at our back when the storms of life blow cold and high, and the inner storms can be some of the worst.

What if the man, the father of our child, the one we thought would be a tree to shelter in when the rains blew cold, has not the strength to be leant on? What of us then?

So what was it like for me, when my own time came to cross the Rubicon and move from being a grown-up child of a parent to being a parent of a child, a new life to which I would be the guardian?

Before it faded too much I wrote a letter, a letter to my son and all sons to try and tell you . . .

My son, I will call you 'little one', because so you are now, though when you read this letter you will be the man that you are travelling day by day to become.

So, to the man that you and I do not know and to other men who may read this . . . what shall I say? Sit down for a little space and listen. You may see the shadow, catch a glimpse of the picture, feel for a moment the weight on your stomach and under your bones.

What was it like to carry this body: to carry another's beginnings? I do not know what men say amongst themselves when they see a woman heavy and swollen by the creation curled within her. Some may turn away, so used to the slender shape put before them on posters and TV screen that they are sickened by the thickness of the lines, the weight of the curve, the fullness of the belly. Others may be fascinated, awed, or full of fear . . . I do not know. I have not heard the thoughts men think before such women . . . I hardly know my own.

You may hear some men say or write that women are blessed, that they turn within themselves to contemplate the miracle that has visited them, that grows within their skin. But I did not glory and rejoice as you were made. Shrouded by my flesh you were spun; life from my life, your flesh teased out and shaped from my bones and blood. Hidden in the dark; month by month, the intricate mystery that is you was drawn from my strength, cell from cell.

I felt so sick, so very, very sick, sick to the depths, weak and longing to sleep, longing for the world to go away. But I was not ill. I was well, they said, a wealthy woman of the West.

'Ah, Mrs Talbot, that's fine, everything's coming along

fine . . . blood pressure's normal . . . weight gain's fine . . . good, good, see you same time next week.'

The kindly doctor's face nodded and smiled me out of her surgery, but there was no word for me . . . only for you, my son, were the careful checks made, the tests taken.

'Good, good, the baby's doing fine . . . Yes, I can feel the spine . . . the heart's beating well . . . See you same time next week, Mrs . . . er . . . yes, Mrs Talbot. Don't forget two pounds a week gain is about the right amount, we can't have you falling behind now, can we?'

I was a would-be mother and all that was now important was the welfare of my child. All the scientific care was for you; for your growing, hidden, tiny body. No one thought that I, struggling to keep my head above the sickness and the fear that sometimes swirled in my stomach, needed a different form of help and one so easily given: a little time, a face that truly listened. The unspoken request for help withered pathetically in the bright beam of the professional smile.

'Morning sickness!' You will hear women and books talk of it, dismissing it by its label . . . morning sickness! It lasted all day! To reach home after a day at work, I had to will each foot in front of the other. I felt quite sorry for my feet. I am sure you will laugh at such a thought . . . but I did.

'Just you keep going,' I would say. 'That's it . . . one in front of the other . . . just you keep at it . . . and we will get there, yes, we will. I know you don't feel as if you'll make it, but just another, a little step, such a little step, one or two will do . . . don't think about that half hour journey . . . just one more step. Don't think. Just another and we're bound to get there . . . in the end . . .'

And of course, we did make it, my feet and I.

After that were the four flights of stairs to our attic flat.

I draped the exhausted, sick, weak body with its growing bump over whatever was nearest, bed or chair. 'Pregnancy . . . a time of expectancy.' There wasn't even the energy to laugh cynically . . .

You lived on the simplest food, my son, in those first eight months of life—you didn't quite make it to the ninth month, but that bit comes a little later. We ate boiled eggs . . . toast . . . and fruit . . . and, oh yes, I mustn't forget that essential ingredient for the making of young bones and teeth must I? Milk . . . how the stuff sickened me! But I drank the thick, white, heavy liquid, sip by nauseous sip. Week after week, month after month, the sickness lay curled upon my days, sometimes heavier, sometimes lighter, but always there, until the second that your tiny, wet, exhausted body slid from my own, then the weight was lifted and was gone. Funny, the minute you were out I felt myself again, free for a little while . . .

I was afraid, my little one, of what it would mean for me, when you decided to move from the inside of things to the outer, oh, so much more difficult world you live in now.

So I thought on God: the beginning and ending of all living things . . . on words from the book of books. 'Her time had not yet come . . . as a woman groans in travail . . . a woman if she perseveres in faith and prayer will be saved in the birth of children.'

I began to think that the saving might be a very literal one!

What would it be like? I asked myself as I had watched, with what I had hoped was a suitable impassive expression, as a young woman with a white, shocked face, was wheeled down from the delivery room to her bed. I can see her face now, paper-pale and pinched in round the nose and mouth. Although I kept my rounded, heavy outer body still, inside my heart shivered and shook.

How would I cope? Would I be overwhelmed, engulfed by pain that was beyond myself? What would it be really like?

So at the heart of the mystery, at the centre what was it like?

At midnight I was summoned by the sound of a pistol shot. Really, that was what it was like but only I heard it: a sound of warning, a crack of an alarm, the beginning of a desperate race. A pain took my breath away and, bent double with it, I staggered, ignominiously dripping water, clutching my nightie round my non-existent waist, down the two flights of stairs to the toilet. As the water round you drained away, the sharp stab twisted and thrust, then paused.

Your father washed his hair. I got my bag together . . . first babies were said to be slow affairs, were they not? But within the hour the pains were every three minutes and before I had drawn breath the next was upon me.

There was no time for the general labour ward—I went straight to the delivery room. Then time and life were concentrated on not being utterly swamped and mentally flung hither and thither by the pains that felt as if they were pulling me apart. The force of them was so big, so beyond myself and yet within me; so merciless and yet neutral: the immense powers within the universe and within my body pushing a new life out into the world. Keeping my inner self somehow above it was a major endeavour . . . to keep above it and yet go with it, that was a task indeed.

'She's certainly having good contractions!'

'Contractions!' I thought, looking at the still, brittle face of the staff nurse.

'Rubbish! It's pain. P.A.I.N. Why don't they call it what it is?'

It's strange, little one. When you are young you feel

much older. Now I am older I feel strangely young. Once upon a time I had thought that life and death were opposites, two ends of a spectrum, two opposing forces. I had not expected that, enfolded within the bearing of your beginning, was an experience that would alter how I felt about dying. I tell you . . . whatever and whoever God is, He is full of surprises. You can work out overall patterns but individual experience takes us by surprise and has the power to astonish.

The experience came unbidden and was certainly, in the midst of all the drama and crisis of the delivery room, distinctly unexpected. It lasted only a very few seconds and yet it has changed my life.

I'm sure you will find it hard to believe but sometimes when I remember and when the other world, with its fragrance of Narnia, draws close, I quite look forward to dying. Like birth, I know that it will be one of the most profound and, dare I say it, one of the most interesting experiences of my life . . .

So how did it all begin, this experience that changed my understanding so radically?

The tremendous force and power of your coming suddenly went awry. You kept your shoulder turned against the outside world and all was changed. I knew that I was in an extreme state and that I was in danger. It was at that moment of extremity that a strange quiet grew from the core of my inner self, grew and enlarged until there were two selves: an inner and an outer. The body that was mine was going through what appeared to be something akin to convulsions but now there was no pain and within a world of quietness I heard a still, small voice speak.

One day, my son, I will read you the story of Elijah who also heard a still, small voice . . . I wonder if the voice is the same.

What did it sound like? . . . It was so clear, so like hearing a human voice, so very, very like, but it was a hearing that was somehow on the inside. Without the help of my ears, words were suddenly there in my mind that I had not gone through the bother of actually thinking . . . it was . . . it was a warning, a preparation, a strange encouragement.

'As *this* is, so your dying will be . . .'

That was all . . . so little and yet so much.

For in that hearing was also a knowing: that all this was for Life; that there were two realities, the inner and the outer; that what things looked like on the outside was not necessarily what was going on on the inside; that both realities were true. There was the body in extremity but the inner self was in a world of quiet, waiting; waiting for the life to be born. That time I was waiting for you, the next time it would be my life that would be waiting to be born, to be pushed by the processes of dying into life. I would be awaiting and struggling to my own beginning.

How you were eventually brought on to planet Earth was a tragedy of mismanagement and errors of judgement, that resulted in the straining, heaving help of forceps. I have wondered then and since what it was like for you to be dragged so unwillingly forth.

At some inner limit point I prayed, 'Please, please, let this time be the last, before something breaks that will never be mended let him come now . . . Please, please let this be the last . . .' And in the mercy of God it was. The new life that was you spilled out in a rush of blood, your tiny limbs disjointed and hanging like a discarded doll; the compact, puppy face turning from the light, bruised and livid from the steel grasp that had hauled you forth . . . my first born son . . .

Chapter 18

Can it be that in the bearing of a new life, a new world, a new consciousness, we women touch upon a thread that runs through the material and spiritual universe; that in pain and danger and physical extremity, new life is born? In our bent world, waiting for the revealing of the children of light, we all have a time to walk our *via dolorosa*, that out of the darkness of our pain, something new, fresh, unique may be born . . . the old books may tell it true.

Seven years on now, and in the throes of a different birth, I begin to see correspondences, that although I feel are profoundly true, I know myself reluctant fully to acknowledge. Just as a birth may not be a consciously willed event in the inner lives of the partners to it, so the birth of a different inner world may come through circumstances that, at least at first, are not of our conscious choosing.

In the forces that were unleashed at my son's birth was a power and a knowledge and a pattern, that broke down the walls of my apparent safety, and I was nearly swept away by the force of the tidal wave that rolled past the flattened defences. I have often wondered why the rescue so often comes at the fifty-ninth minute of the eleventh hour, leaving us gasping, dazed and maybe very much afraid, having just looked a very different dying full in the face . . .

I think perhaps if the rescue came sooner, we would never learn of the outer and inmost reaches of the self. We would never choose to explore the darkest areas of shadow in the border country between death and life . . . and yet that land is there. It is worth exploring and signposts need to be set up there for the human wanderer just as in any other part of the universe that we inhabit. The hidden continent within needs its pioneers and explorers and, like the wanderer in the Minotaur's maze, we need the scarlet thread to guide us, so that we can find the way forward as well as back.

The third time that I have come to that border country in which the shadows of death and life meet each other was, and is, in a different kind of dying altogether . . . I am still in that border area, but at the eleventh hour I was not left to wander in the dark alone. Companions and a guide have been given to help me in my search for the way out of the maze in the land of the shadow, and in my hand is the scarlet thread to mark the way . . . a reminder that is both a warning and a safety as I search for the inner way to freedom.

Most dying, it seems to me, is a messy, painful, complex process. Dying and rebirth is not a simple before-and-after process; the spiritual principle echoes the process and difficulty of the physical. It is not something that you can short-circuit. If a short cut is attempted, an abortive or damaged creation is the most likely result.

In this third, so different birth and death process, I begin to catch a glimpse at the core of the pain, of a call to a different kind of life; to a different knowledge of loving; to a different experience of womanhood, that I believe has the power to reorder my inner and outer worlds. I am not there yet but, like Christian on his journey, I have caught a sight of the Delectable Mountains and beyond them the light of the Celestial City, which gives me the strength—just—to continue the search. I do not feel that it is better to travel hopefully than to arrive, rather one can only travel hopefully if there is some conviction of the possibility of a destination worth the reaching . . .

When now I interview for the radio and someone talks to me of principles, again and again and again I ask, 'yes . . . but what exactly do you mean? Can you describe to me what happened and how . . .?'

It is time for me to answer my own questions . . .

What was it like for me? What was the process actually like . . . the death of a dream; of a sacred dream; of the marriage that held me?

'Divorce . . .' I really didn't think that it would happen to me, that I would be one of the one in three for whom marriage dies. After all, the invisible third, divine presence that accompanied us along our way, surely, surely, He would guard me from such disaster. So I had hoped. I forgot that that divine third is inextricably and in essence bound up with truth and life. He does not tolerate anything but that which is true and living in those who are seriously following the mystic way. But oh, I did not think that I would end up a statistic—a casualty on a list!

So to my son and to all sons and daughters of mothers and to the mothers of sons and daughters for whom the mercy and grace of life has spared the knowledge and experience that has come perforce to me . . . I write to tell you how it was, and I hope and pray that in the struggle of the living and the telling, a seeing may begin and in the seeing, the life of a different sort of knowing and understanding.

My dear son, there was a few weeks' respite, after you had come to this planet . . . a few precious weeks of days rocking your basket, awed at this little self, rump stuck in the air like a flag; black, feathery hair and minute fists, clutching at nothingness. You whimpered as you slept but the touch and stroke of a hand would soothe it away for a while, for such a little while . . .

I felt so utterly privileged to care for you, my little one, my son. I can see and feel you now, a little lump in your sling, sleeping high on my stomach between my breasts, cuddled close, so small, so utterly defenceless . . .

Oh, how to tell you of the rest?

It was a cold winter that year, the worst for many, many years. Snow and ice congealed, blinding the windows, shutting us in . . . and you cried, hour after hour. Day after day you wailed and wept at the life to which you had come.

I tried everything, did everything the books had said. In your special chair you accompanied me everywhere I went. I was never without you. If left even for a second, the weeping turned to screams of desperation.

The house was bare, cold, full only of dust, standing thick in the air; dirt ingrained on floorboards and doors. Everywhere was grey, seamed with dirt, negligence, disorder and decay. Old plaster-pock-marked walls glared greyly, balefully hostile to us both, these new inhabitants, so desperate, so innocent, so alone.

You cried and cried my strength away. And the crying came along the line of a geographical fault within the rock of the self. The sound vibrated along the lines of scar tissue and I was undefended.

Nappies lay in soggy heaps, frosted in the grimy cold. I stared at them, too weary, too tired to wash them. The next day they were there still, the danger signs unseen by my lover, my husband: for your father was away in search of himself. And so we were left, you and I. The hours crawled by on hurting feet.

The weariness became flecked and stained with rage. I longed to break and tear the grey, cold-weeping walls that gave me no rest, no comfort, no respite. I was left to cope alone, as is the assigned lot of women. When your father came in so late, so very late, I longed to shake and shake him till there was no breath left in him; to shout and scream and beat the air until he could feel my pain.

I tried once to tell him, but his ears could not hear, for he was, he hoped, at the beginning of his dream; the bright lights were shining and the smell of greasepaint was in his nostrils: his name was on the programme. And babies cried, after all, did they not? Women through the ages had dealt with these things and so would I. I was the strong one, after all. The dirt . . . the mess? In a little time, when he had time, it would be better, but he was so busy, so tired . . .

So I shouted and swore to the empty air and waiting walls, hurting my throat with my screams and then feeling such a fool, but such a desperate, helpless fool.

And you, frightened at my fury, cried all the more. Begging and pleading you to stop—knowing that you could not understand and that such pleading, like all else, could only fail—I shook and shook you. Fear, little one, changed your cry. Instead of anger, frustration and pain rolled into one retching, rhythmic moan; you wept and saved yourself. So we wept together, you and I, and your hair was soaked by my fear.

I picked you up and together we fled the house.

Tears streaming down my face, I knocked on a neighbour's door. She was a mother. For many years she had reared a child (now grown), alone. No words were needed. She knew . . . 'Come in. Come in . . .' she said. 'Have a nice cup of tea and you'll soon feel better.' We came in and in the coming-in, in our welcome, was the power to stop your crying—for that day and for that moment of danger at least.

They said that after four to five months your crying would stop. It didn't but the quality was changed. You no longer cried in pain, but retched and whimpered, caught in some as then unknown tension and frustration that knew no release. You were imprisoned and I with you. I did not have the wisdom then to set you free . . . and in that lack of knowledge was a terrible danger.

And so, my little one, the months passed by. The weather changed slowly and we would walk, filling the days, your crying eased for a little by the constant changing scene before your new eyes; but the cold, the leaden skies, began to colour the inner horizon behind my eyes, so that all was grey and turned to stone.

I became a Midas of granite and ash: all I touched turning to cinders of cries and ashes at my leaden feet.

In the first few years of your life, my son, I lost myself: the self that was not mother, not wife, and in that losing I nearly chose to lose my life . . . nearly but not quite, because in the end we all find what we truly seek.

I went in search of her, the woman I had lost. I searched through months and days of pain, but as in all the old stories, if you search with all your heart you find. In the end we all find what we truly seek and it isn't always what we expect. But oh, my son, in that losing, although as with all endings it held within it the seed of a new finding, I lost my lover and you a father who in flesh was near. But in that ending, as in all endings, there is for us both a beginning. It is always so. But we need courage and strength and will to persevere so that we may fully find it and be found . . .

Oh my son, my son, I have longed, as you may one day long, to count in a special way: to be at the pivot point in another's life and I to be central to his. I have longed to share the triumphs, the pain and the little things, from sunsets to rainbows to dealing with the rising damp! Oh it's not good for man to be alone, nor for woman either! Perhaps it is not good particularly for woman, because we have been made so much to see our meaning in relationship to another. I begin to wonder whether, within the tragic death of the stability of the family and of the marriages that create it, is a call, a challenge, particularly to women.

Maybe Christ is calling us and perhaps particularly the many, many women who face a life of singleness not chosen: to find in the dying of the dream a freedom.

The gauntlet has been thrown down at our feet and the Divine Other waits to see how we will respond to the challenge to find a centre from within: a stability and a strength that may be discovered at the heart of the self and from the core of Life that we call God: to find on behalf of all women a new way of living.

It is interesting that Christ, although surrounded by people and having the capacity to love and understand that went beyond us all, never married. 'As the Father has life in Himself, so He has given to the Son to have life in Himself.' It is to discover that life from within the centre of the self and not derived from work or children or husband that I search on the inner way.

Oh my son . . . I remember how, in a church alive with flowers and my man waiting for me at the porch with a yellow flower in his waistband and a waiting silence that was thick under the drumming of the rain on the roof, I thought that in the speaking of the marriage vow before a crowd of witnesses and before the silent heavens, that with this man, this lover by my side and I at his, I would no longer be alone. I thought I would be no longer oppressed or afraid, when facing that sense of being in a silence so immense, in a universe so beautiful, so strange, so intricate and so other. No, I thought, I was no longer on my own: a struggling speck of humanity on the face of the earth. I thought . . . I thought, that on this day, my wedding day, this aloneness would die.

I could not have been more wrong.

Marriage being a thing of life: a living, growing, spiritual link between two mysterious beings, like all things of life it can grow alongside the lives of the people who feed it. And like all growing things, it can sicken and die and the light die with it, until the sun rises again upon an apparently dead and barren land and the soil is loosened to make way for new shoots of a different growth.

That decision, my son, spoken in the marriage vow: to be committed to find the way of loving, no matter what, must be renewed each day. And what of us, my little one, if that decision day by day begins to die, when the clouds within and without are grey and full of rain?

It is like a bad dream. We hope we will wake up but know that we will not . . . that now the nightmare is for real and there will be no waking. We will have to live through it; the whirlwind's ahead and we must go through the eye of the storm. In all the most difficult things of life that is the way of it . . . the only way of escape is to go wide-eyed and awake through the very worst and find what is on the other side of tears.

Eventually the moment comes from which there is no turning back. When these words were spoken to the air I did not expect them. 'I've been thinking,' said my man, with his arm across his face so that he did not have to see the living pain of the woman he had called wife. 'I've been thinking . . . perhaps I will move out for a few weeks, go and stay with a friend . . .'

And then the agony of Solomon's choice . . . How can a child be in two places at one time?

I was so cold I shook, but I was determined not to be seen to shake. I heard my voice say, 'I've lost my work. I'm losing you . . . please don't take my child as well, just when it's getting better, him and me . . . Don't take everything . . .'

I walked the streets and when I lay down again I clung to the side of the bed as though it were the edge of a precipice, and I was so cold; I went to sleep like a tramp huddled in an old dressing-gown under the quilt, shivering like a dog in a storm.

I was not left utterly forsaken; the words I had read, that a smoking flax would not be quenched, are true. Help came in all sorts of different ways. Sometimes the love of Christ smiles at us through the welcome of an invitation to dinner, through the love of the natural family, or even in the gaiety of a squirrel scrambling up a tree. Sometimes at times of great grief, the phone has rung unexpectedly at unusual times . . . and a friend's voice has said, 'Are you all right? I just had this feeling that I needed to phone you . . .', and in that contact I knew myself not to be alone.

The months passed. The agony of what to do, or what not to do, went on. I had made a vow . . . a life-long vow, but I could not be married to a man who did not live with me, whom I had begun to realise had found another, a young girl who would help him refind the youth he had lost.

I was neither married nor free. The waiting and the tension of uncertainty stretched before me through uncounted years. It was like being stretched upon a rack.

I will never forget the day I stopped praying that somehow the Spirit of God would bring my husband back. I turned my back on all the advice that was given from within the orthodox Church . . . do nothing . . . and in time . . . in time all would be made well . . . In one thing they were right. In time all will be made well but not in the way they thought. I prayed for the first time that I would be able to hear what the word of Christ was for me in the Now, to be able to hear, whatever that word was . . . to be able to hear it and know it. That was all. It was enough . . .

A strange silence grew. It stood: a standing stillness. The stillness waited. For the first time in months I was inwardly stilled, and in that calm I went upstairs, thinking at least I would sleep tonight. As I opened the door the standing stillness was there to greet me: a presence; a waiting. Then it spoke. Not in words that the air could hear, but words that spoke themselves somehow, just on the edge of sound.

It was a question. An enquiry. 'Could I? Would I?' said the Voice, 'Could I divorce John out of love, not hate? As a last act of love, should it become necessary, if it was finally asked of me . . . could I release him from his vow? Let him go free?'

It was the last thing I could give him . . . his freedom.

The standing stillness waited. The column of quietness stood to listen to what I would say.

I was utterly free to decide. So I thought of the man I loved . . . and what could be said but, 'Yes'. And to the God I loved, to the hidden Christ who asked . . . what could be said but 'Yes'.

'But oh, what will become of me?' I asked. I knew I was not as strong as I seemed. 'What will become of me?' I asked the waiting quiet. But there was no answer. Only a waiting—a waiting and a watching.

Weeping I went through the darkened house; my grief wept to the silent doors and walls.

In the days that followed I prayed to understand what I had experienced, and during a sermon in church that inner voice spoke again, quite separate from what was outwardly going on.

'You see,' it said, 'it's like the story of Jeptha . . . who vowed a vow, that if he won the victory in battle the first living thing that greeted him would be sacrificed to God . . . and that living thing was his own daughter. And in his reverence for the vow he took the life of a living being . . .'

I am a Jew. I understand this deep reverence for the Law . . . for the vow. The Law has within it something of the nature of God.

'But you see,' went on the inner teacher. 'If you hold on to the letter of the law, to the vow, without the inner spiritual reality of which the vow should speak, you create a dead thing . . . like Jeptha. Have you forgotten what you have been told . . . that the letter of the Law kills, but the Spirit gives life?

* * *

So now I stand in a keener wind. There is no one at my back and I know I must face the question of my life alone in the light of those turning stars . . . and that the hidden Christ who is Truth and Freedom and Life itself will be with me in my search to do more than endure . . . but rather deeply and truly . . . to live.

Chapter 19

For five years I have sought to do more than endure. I have searched to find the way to the other side of grief, to know and discover the resurrection of a self that had died, lost in the ashes of some of the hopes and dreams that I had dreamed when I was young.

Oh, I had wished with a wish like in the fairy stories of my youth, to re-make what had been broken. I had hoped for a lover and husband who would show me that a man could love differently, with gentleness and strength. I wanted to create a family and a marriage that would bring warmth and life and love and laughter to me and the children that might come from the centre of such a living. I had wanted to use the warmth from my hearth's fire to warm others, who might be weary and cold on their journey's way. Such was the dream and such is the dream that draws on so many to try again to re-create a pattern worth the making.

What I didn't know then was that to choose an over-gentle man is to choose a man who is unable to inherit his strength, whose strength has gone underground, whose gentleness may disguise tension and repression and fear. In my choosing I was not free as I chose in direct reaction to the shadow of my father. Even in that I was patterned by his life.

Yet the power that works for our good knows these things. Through the myriad layers of unknowing and the patterning of the past upon us can come wisdom, knowledge and freedom. Most things of great value are not bought cheaply. The old legends often talk of the treasure being gained only after trial, tribulations and many testings; so it is with the treasures of the spirit.

There have been times when the longing for the dream that was, the grief of its ending and my own abandonment were so great that I stumbled through days in a haze of pain. My body ached with a weight of sorrow so heavy that I hardly had energy to walk or speak. I prayed and thought and searched, refusing to shed tears so that they solidified into a stone that seemed to sap even the will to live. At my centre was a pain that was also a hole, through which the life blood seemed to flow away. I felt like a body without strength that mechanically got itself through the days . . . just.

What was to be done?

I found that prayer and fasting would bring temporary relief. Suddenly I could breathe easy again. The inner stone was rolled away and for a while I lived again. Yet always the pain returned; a groaning ache at the centre.

For three years I waited. I would not go the way of my father. Not for me the array of magic rainbow pills. Somehow I would find my way, my very own way, directed, I hoped against hope, by a wisdom that lay at the heart of life. Again I encountered the mystery of the triple three. At the end of the three years I knew I needed help. I could not go it alone. I needed a guide through the labyrinthine ways of heart and mind. If God was God and the source of all wisdom, there must be a right way for me; a way through and beyond where I was.

I looked and searched, listened and waited. At least I had learnt something. I had learned not to rush. I had learned to wait. So I waited; waited for the Teacher; waited for a guide to be put in my path.

There is a Zen saying that the Master and the Disciple wander through the world and when they meet they recognise eath other. . . .

It's funny the things that create a meeting point. For me it was being flattened by hay-fever of all things! That particular summer it was so bad that the only relief was to lie down in a darkened room; a soggy flannel over my face and protesting nose!

The discomfort became the means by which I was given an impetus to consider a course of action that I would not normally have taken. Through coincidence of events, a friendship and a common interest in art, a fellow-traveller on the Christ way had mentioned in the passing conversation a doctor who practised psychotherapy. I learnt that this woman also had a love of art and a great interest in the ways of mind and spirit. Although trained in the NHS, she now practised in Homoeopathy. Sneezing my way to her door I wondered through swollen eyes whether perhaps this was the teacher that I sought. It was not the most auspicious of beginnings.

I was loth to begin. In the secret of my heart I asked for a sign, coward that I was. I needed some indication whether this was the place that I might begin my journey. The sign that was particular to me was given; such a tiny, small thing it was, yet within myself I knew.

I was called within to adventure forth on a strange, disquieting, mysterious and mystical journey . . . 'to explore the dark continent within . . .'

Laughingly to friends I have called it the 'magical-mystery-mystical-tour . . .' imagining it like the Beatles film, *The Yellow Submarine*, in which you never quite knew what would float into view next, and 'dark' was not perhaps quite the right adjective!

'But what was it like this journey?' I can hear you say. I am too near the beginning yet to describe it clearly. I can only as yet give hints, rough outlines and smudges of colour that might suggest some sense of its character and quality. It certainly has its own patterns, currents and mode of operation. One of the main ones being surprise! A mystery journey indeed! I never quite know where I am going or where I will end up.

But in it and through it all one thing has already been made plain: the way beyond the pain was to agree to go through it; to let things happen. What was needed it seemed was freely, through the will, to take the decision to let the pain take you to its heart; to allow oneself to experience in full what lay hidden, bunched and knotted and put aside for so many years.

At the eye of the storm, beyond the tears that might wrack the body and exhaust the mind there is a stillness. And in that stillness came a truth that like all truth held within it the power to set free. But it is not easy to look truth in the face—like all things to do with the gods it can make us afraid.

For me, the 'continent within' was not unlike some of the terrain I had discovered in the journey of prayer. In fact, the one experience so closely allied the other that it was difficult to distinguish the one *from* the other. In both was the experience of having my perceptions reorganised; a call beyond pain to a different type of seeing; a different type of knowing. I began to realise that all things were not without significance, including our likes and dislikes and that what we resisted most might be the thing that we most needed to examine.

I had to be willing to go along different routes; to give up old ways of thinking; to try new actions both inner and outer.

One thing I resisted above every other was the idea and practical suggestion that it might help the process if I lay down . . .' The idea filled me with horror and revulsion.

I would do no such thing. No way! Absolutely not!

'Why not?' my teacher asked.

I thought and considered and pulled a few good reasons from my mind.

'Do you feel good not being able to do something?'

I did not. The gauntlet was thrown down. I picked it up and considered the question anew. It could perhaps be quite interesting to discover what lay behind that distaste. The lying down of my body might lead me to it. As in all things I was free to choose. I could choose to explore or not. I decided to discover what patterns might be found in the experience of the horizontal.

It was strong medicine. I had had good reason to be so resistant to lying down.

In some of that discovery lay an experience of listening to and looking at images that I knew were from my racial past. I had not lived them and yet they were there: stark, demanding to be considered. For the first time in twenty years I looked them straight in the face. It was not a pleasant sight.

Image after image of horror and massacre rose to the surface of my mind. Burning villages and pathetic, twisting bundles of bodies, turned and turned, suspended from trees before my sickened gaze.

In and through it all was the challenge to integrate this also. This that was not me and yet also was a part of what I was and am. In the land of the spirit, past, present and future can change places with the most dizzy-making effect.

Lying down, I recalled again the memory of my father coming to my room when I was a child and lying alongside me in the bed. Nothing outwardly was wrong and yet I knew then without words, as children do, that this was not right; that he sought from me something I did not understand and that I knew I could not give.

I have said at the beginning of this story that this account in some ways is the story of a father and a daughter and in some ways it is. But it is also a seeking of the way beyond the shadow that was within him, that covered us both like a cloak, binding me to his pattern.

Truth revealed can enable us to choose freedom.

And what of my father? He thought that through change of woman he could change the pattern of his inner pain. He could not. Like so many men he chose to see the problems as outside himself and so the pattern was repeated. Again the violence, the SOS emergency calls, the coming of the doctor and the police.

And now? Now, he sits in a room, blanketed around with his longing for a love that I cannot give; a longing and a yearning for the accepting love of a mother who could not love the boy that he was. The shadow covers him still.

Last year I told him that the only thing I could do for him now was to find my own way, because that could be peace to him too. I was so nearly overcome. It was no good the two of us drowning together in the name of family and kinship loyalty. One of us had to strike out to the shore. Then may be I could throw him a rope and see if he would take it.

Sometimes refusal can be another way to life and a 'No' may have its place in the pattern. . . .

Christ said some dreadfully unsettling, devastating things. To the man who said he could not follow this prophet of Nazareth until his parents no longer needed him, this revolutionary of the Spirit said, 'Let the dead bury the dead . . . Come and follow me . . .'.

The love and call of God can be terrible things. It is indeed a terrible thing to fall into the hands of the living God. The writer to the Hebrews knew what he was talking about.

Postscript

It is five years now, five the number of division and creation . . . and in the ending of that dream of marriage and the safety that I thought it brought, begins a new shoot of life; the emerging of a deeper, stronger, bigger, more dangerous and challenging dream that has been with me since I was a child. For many years it was with me, partly hidden, divided into many facets. Now it has emerged. In the breaking of the glass the genii is out of the bottle.

Whether I have the strength and the will to give the dream its life: to give it flesh and bones and blood, so that it can stand and take its place in the world, I do not know—yet. But I know that I will have no rest until I have lent it all the strength I have . . . until I have tried and tried and tried, using all the skill of waiting that I have learnt in the desert years. I do not know yet but I will find out . . .

Meanwhile, there are still the days of pain . . . of waking in the night with the bed too wide, the house too quiet and only the alarm clock to wake me in the morning. But then there comes another day, another sort of day altogether, and with it the hope that soon . . . in just a little while, I will be on the other side of grief.

In this other day I get up to an empty house, no, not empty: a house full of quiet and colour and a calm waiting. I wake and see the light through the curtains and realise that today, at last, at long, long last the ache at the centre of my body is not there . . . the dread and fear of another day to be got through, to drag my weary body and aching heart through, that ache is gone. This day is different. And why is this day different? Oh, only for a small reason that can change the world. I am different.

I come into my bedroom and see the dapple-light-sun gleam and shine from wall and polished-wood-bed. The colour of the rug glows like stained glass.

It is good to be alive.